MEDICAL CONDITIONS AFFECTING DRIVERS

Theodore C. Doege and Alan L. Engelberg, Editors

American Medical Association

First Printing   1986

Additional copies may be purchased from:
Order Department   OP-018
American Medical Association
P.O. Box 10946
Chicago, Illinois 60610-0946

HDG:86:634:2M:11/86

MEDICAL CONDITIONS AFFECTING DRIVERS

Table of Contents

CONTRIBUTORS

James L. Breeling - Scientist-Medical Writer, Division of Clinical Science, American Medical Association, Chicago, Illinois.

Francis I. Catlin, M.D., Sc.D. - Professor, Otorhinolaryngology and Communicative Sciences, Baylor College of Medicine, Houston, Texas.

Theodore C. Doege, M.D., M.S. - Special Advisor-Science and Senior Scientist, American Medical Association, Chicago, Illinois; Associate Professor, Epidemiology-Biometry Program, School of Public Health, University of Illinois at Chicago.

John W. Eberhard, Ph.D. - Senior Research Psychologist, Office of Driver and Pedestrian Research, National Highway Traffic Safety Administration, Washington, D.C.

Alan L. Engelberg, M.D., M.P.H. - Director, Department of Public Health, and Senior Scientist, American Medical Association, Chicago, Illinois.

Thomas C. Gibson, M.B. - Professor, Department of Medicine, University of Vermont College of Medicine, Burlington, Vermont.

Lee N. Hames - President, Health and Safety Associates, Inc., Deerfield, Illinois; Managing Editor, Quarterly/Journal, American Association for Automotive Medicine, Arlington Heights, Illinois.

David L. Horwitz, M.D. - Clinical Associate Professor, Section of Endocrinology, Department of Medicine, University of Illinois Health Sciences Center, Chicago, Illinois.

Arthur H. Keeney, M.D., Sc.D. - Professor and Interim Chairman, Department of Ophthalmology; Dean Emeritus, University of Louisville School of Medicine, Louisville, Kentucky.

Russell Noyes, Jr., M.D. - Professor of Psychiatry, Department of Psychiatry, University of Iowa College of Medicine, Iowa City, Iowa.

Charles M. Poser, M.D. - Lecturer on Neurology, Harvard Medical School; Attending Neurologist, Beth Israel Hospital, Boston, Massachusetts.

John D. States, M.D. - Professor and Chairman, Department of Orthopedics, Rochester General Hospital and University of Rochester School of Medicine and Dentistry, Rochester, New York.

Jeffery M. Stokols, J.D. - Assistant Director, Department of State Legislation, American Medical Association, Chicago, Illinois.

Arthur A. Tritsch - Director, Driver Services, American Association of Motor Vehicle Administrators, Washington, D.C.

Alexander C. Wagenaar, Ph.D. - Associate Research Scientist, Systems Analysis Division, University of Michigan Transportation Research Institute, Ann Arbor, Michigan.

Julian A. Waller, M.D., M.P.H. - Professor, Department of Medicine, University of Vermont College of Medicine, Burlington, Vermont.

James L. Weygandt, M.D. - Occupational Physician, Kohler Company, Kohler, Wisconsin.

Robert T. Willis, M.D. - Department of Medicine, The Sheboygan Clinic, Sheboygan, Wisconsin.

Preface

Since the 1920s when its House of Delegates recommended examinations to determine drivers' fitness, the American Medical Association has been concerned with highway safety issues. During recent decades, committees of the Association have had leadership roles in devising the Abbreviated Injury Scale, advocating the installation of seat belts in new automobiles, and defining intoxication of the driver, all of which are important matters pertaining to highway safety.

The first AMA publication on medical conditions of drivers appeared in 1959. After it underwent several revisions, most recently in 1973, it seemed appropriate to review this important subject. Those selected to help with the task were persons knowledgeable about injuries on the highway and their causes, certain kinds of medical problems, and state and federal licensing requirements. Their efforts led to this book, which has received the endorsement of the AMA's Council on Scientific Affairs.

The contributors and editors acknowledge the assistance of many AMA staff members who assisted with this publication. Leonard D. Fenninger, M.D. and Philip L. White, Sc.D. authorized beginning the task, and M. Roy Schwarz, M.D. and William R. Hendee, Ph.D. provided strong impetus toward its completion. We especially thank Barbara S. Jansson, who prepared the final manuscript, and Leatha A. Tiggelaar, Elaine Tejcek and Rita M. Palulonis, who handled many tasks associated with the publication.

Theodore C. Doege, M.D., M.S.
Alan L. Engelberg, M.D., M.P.H.

Chapter 1

INTRODUCTION: DRIVING AND CLASSIFYING DRIVERS

Few technologic developments influence the lives of Americans as much as motor vehicles. The distances that must be traveled in this nation in order to attend an educational institution, earn a living, spend leisure time or visit the physician often are great; yet responsible drivers and good motor vehicles and highways can neutralize these distance-isolation factors. Because Americans spend so much time driving, they inevitably are exposed to the risk of crashes and fatal injuries. But there is evidence that the risk of such injuries has been decreasing since the 1930s (1,2).

Like most Americans, physicians want to help impaired persons participate fully in the educational, occupational, recreational, social and other activities of our society. No physician without good reason should recommend depriving an impaired patient of the privilege of driving. Yet the physician should be equally reluctant to recommend driving if it puts the patient or others of the community at serious risk of injury because of a crash. Such injuries constitute one of the nation's most significant health problems and can lead to long-term physical and mental residua as well as to temporary impairment.

Safe operation of a motor vehicle is a demanding task that requires physical and mental capabilities sufficient to control a machine weighing one or more tons and easily capable of causing serious injury. The driver must be alert and capable of quick, accurate and appropriate interpretations and judgments about rapidly changing conditions that relate to vehicles, pedestrians, traffic lights, street signs, roads and weather. The driver must be able to act immediately, rapidly and appropriately. Drivers must be in full possession of their senses, especially vision, in order to assimilate, interpret and act according to visual and other cues.

Underscoring the importance of the driver is a well-designed study that examined interactions among human, vehicular and environmental factors in crashes. Drivers' errors were considered to be definite causal factors, defined as being necessary or sufficient for the crashes to occur, in 71% of crashes (3).

What medical conditions can affect a patient's driving and what factors should enter into the physician's recommendations about driving? How can physicians assist administrators of state licensing agencies, who ultimately make decisions about licensing drivers? What is the role of alcohol in crashes? How can physicians aid in the prevention of injuries due to crashes? The purposes of this book are to help answer such questions and to help physicians and others become better informed about such issues.

The contributors to this book exerted much effort to ascertain and describe what is known concerning risks of the more common medical problems as they relate to driving. However, in many instances, unequivocal scientific data are not available concerning the driving performances of persons with such problems. The reader should understand that if references and data to support a specific recommendation do not appear in the text, the recommendation may be based primarily on the judgment and experience of the contributors.

While this book is intended to provide guidance regarding the process to be followed in evaluating patients and making recommendations about reducing the risk of crashes, it cannot provide precise recommendations that can be applied to a specific patient, because each person's circumstances are different and regulations regarding driving and licensing vary from state to state.

With regard to one matter, however, there is uniformity. The Bureau of Motor Carrier Safety of the U.S. Department of Transportation has the authority to regulate medical standards of drivers in interstate commerce (49 CFR Part 391). Practicing physicians should become familiar with those federal regulations if they examine drivers who wish to operate in interstate commerce.

The classification of drivers followed in this book, according to the fitness of drivers in medical terms and according to the types of vehicles they are medically qualified to operate, appears below. The classification is compatible with that recommended by the American Association of Motor Vehicle Administrators and the U.S. Department of Transportation (4), except that the AMA classification places drivers of taxicabs in Class II. According to the AMA classification, drivers with Class I medical qualifications are medically qualified in Classes II and III and drivers in Class II are medically qualified in Class III.

It is important to understand that uniformity does not exist among the states with regard to the medical qualifications of drivers. One state, for example, may require taxi drivers to have medical qualifications similar to those of drivers in Class I, while another state may require them to have medical qualifications of drivers in Class II.

The physician should become familiar with the classifications of the states where his or her patients reside, as well as with special regulations concerning individuals with certain conditions or undergoing certain treatments, because the regulations may affect various aspects of patients' lives, including their occupations. Also, the physician's recommendations and actions should be consistent with those regulations.

Classification of Drivers

Class I: These are drivers who are medically qualified to operate any vehicle, including passenger-carrying vehicles, such as school, charter, city, intrastate and interstate buses; airport limousines and buses; van pools as primary drivers; emergency equipment such as ambulances, fire engines and rescue vehicles; large, heavy articulated trucks and vehicles; and trucks transporting hazardous materials, such as fuel, chemicals, explosives and radioactive substances.

Class II: These are drivers who are medically qualified to operate taxicabs; large non-passenger-carrying vehicles; and trucks, including single vehicles weighing more than 24,000 pounds, and such vehicles towing trailers weighing less than 10,000 pounds.

Class III: These are drivers who are medically qualified to operate personal and private vehicles that are not for hire, do not carry hazardous materials, carry nine people or fewer, and weigh less than 24,000 pounds. The vehicles may tow trailers weighing less than 10,000 pounds that do not carry passengers for hire or hazardous materials and are not used as emergency vehicles.

Persons in the United States continue to benefit from increasing longevity, which means that in coming decades more elderly persons and their physicians will be facing decisions about driving. Older persons may undergo physiologic changes, such as decrease in vision, hearing, strength and coordination. Co-existing chronic conditions can diminish their abilities and reserves. If an illness or injury occurs, the older person is not likely to recover as rapidly as a younger person. However, a diminishing of critical skills is not necessarily automatic (5), nor will it be uniform according to age group, sex and other characteristics.

The physician should attempt to give competent counsel about the advisability of the patient's driving. Yet the physician's obligation is not only to the patient. Physicians also have the ethical obligations of improving the community, respecting the law and applying scientific knowledge (6). Fortunately, as the physician ponders how to advise the patient, helpful information gathered over a period of years may be available to help make the decision. This may include not only data pertaining to past medical history and current health status, but also information received from family members concerning driving and recent illnesses and behavior.

Patients as well as physicians have obligations concerning safety on the road. Specifically, the patient should provide reliable information about past medical history and driving history and accurate information about current use of therapeutic and other kinds of drugs. The patient, not the physician, is in charge of the motor vehicle and ultimately must assume responsibility for his or her own safety and that of people encountered along the way. While eight states require physicians to report certain conditions impairing drivers to state licensing agencies, all states require drivers to notify the agencies if such conditions exist. This emphasizes the primary responsibility of the patient.

A problem facing physicians who wish to make recommendations to their patients about driving is that the biomedical and psychosocial literature does not always provide an unambiguous guide to a course of action. Part of the problem may relate to study designs leading to the collection of data that are less precise than desirable. Another aspect pertains to the definition of "excessive risk." Should drivers with serious medical conditions be measured against the known high risk of male teenagers or against the group with lowest risk, drivers who are 30 to 60 years old? The approach favored in this publication is to measure the crash risks of persons with medical problems against the risk of a crash for the average driver, to maintain surveillance of drivers with medical problems and to deal with progression of their problems as necessary. The practical goal is to reduce the impaired driver's risk of crashes rather than to prevent crashes altogether.

Several well-designed studies suggest that drivers with chronic medical conditions, especially those with alcoholism, have higher crash rates than the rest of the driving public (7). Yet a group of Swedish investigators concluded that persons with conditions such as diabetes mellitus, heart disease, renal disease, deafness and reduced vision were no more likely than drivers without such conditions to have crashes and violations (8).

How strict should the physician be in advising the patient? Most physicians probably are dedicated to reducing risk in a way that is consistent with the patient's maintaining a reasonable life style, rather than to eliminating risk altogether and possibly disrupting the patient's life. It is hoped that such a philosophy would be similar to that of the state's licensing agency.

The presence of a medical diagnosis does not necessarily imply that a patient's driving is affected (9). As physicians know, a diagnosis per se provides little or no insight into how the patient is functioning. Furthermore, even when a moderate degree of functional impairment is judged to exist (10), whether the person is licensed to drive depends on many other factors, such as age, past driving performance and the availability of a vehicle in safe operating condition.

Recommendations about driving are made by physicians to their individual patients, to drivers' licensing agencies, or to both. Although legal decisions about licensing are made by officials of state agencies and not by physicians, the information supplied by physicians should be as complete and accurate as possible to aid the formulation of those decisions. A recently revised publication, "Guides to the Evaluation of Permanent Impairment" (11), can help the physician analyze and accurately measure the impairment of any organ system.

The physician would do well to consider the following pertinent questions before advising the patient about driving:

1. How forthright and reliable is the patient in giving a history? Have sources of information such as relatives and other physicians been consulted?

2. Does the patient have the physical and mental capabilities and characteristics that are needed to drive safely and responsibly?

3. Does the patient have a single medical problem or do several problems exist that together might affect the risk of driving or the safety of others?

4. Would the type and amount of a prescribed medication affect the patient's ability to drive? Would the patient be reliable in taking the medication? Has the patient been advised about the potential effects of the medication on safe driving?

5. What is the patient's driving history? Is driving exposure about average, 10,000 to 15,000 miles per year? Can the patient determine when and where he or she drives or is there little control over the circumstances of driving?

6. Is there a history of previous crashes or moving violations, and what were the circumstances? Does the patient tend to be a "risk taker"?

7. Is there evidence of episodic or chronic impairment due to the abusive use of alcohol, controlled substances or other drugs?

8. What is the prognosis for the patient's medical condition(s) during the period of licensing? For example, are there likely to be changes in the frequency or severity of angina or seizures; in memory, judgment, vision; in strength, stamina or range of motion? Would the changes affect the patient's functioning?

9. Does the patient have an occupation, such as driving a truck, bus or ambulance, that would put many persons at increased risk?

10. Should a driving test be recommended? (12)

It is appropriate that the American Medical Association (AMA) prepare recommendations for physicians concerning medical conditions that may affect drivers, because safety on the highway long has been a concern of the Association. Important publications on the subject that have come from the AMA include a book on the effects of alcohol (13) and a system for classifying crash-related injuries (14). The authors and editors of this publication hope it will uphold that tradition, being useful and informative to all who consider the important matters of whether a person is medically qualified to drive and what risks and hazards might be involved.

References

1. Council on Scientific Affairs: Automobile-related injuries: Components, trends, prevention. JAMA 1983; 249:3216-3222.

2. National Safety Council (NSC): Accident Facts 1983 Edition. Chicago, NSC, 1983.

3. Treat JR: A study of precrash factors involved in traffic accidents. HSRI Res Rev 1980; 10:1-35.

4. National Highway Traffic Safety Administration, U.S. Department of Transportation: Functional Aspects of Driver Impairment. Washington, D.C., U.S. Government Printing Office, 1980.

5. Dans PE, Kerr MR: Gerontology and geriatrics in medical education. New Engl J Med 1979; 300:228-232.

6. American Medical Association: The principles of medical ethics. JAMA 1981; 245:2188.

7. Waller JA: Medical Impairment to Driving. Springfield, IL, Charles C. Thomas, 1973.

8. Ysander L: The safety of drivers with chronic disease. Brit J Indus Med 1966; 23:28-36.

9. Waller JA: Functional impairment in driving. New York State J Med 1980; December, pp 1987-1991.

10. Hales RH: Functional ability profiles for driver licensing. Arch Ophthalmol 1982;100:1780-1783.

11. American Medical Association (AMA): Guides to the Evaluation of Permanent Impairment (2nd Ed). Chicago, American Medical Association, 1984, pp 225-226.

12. Russell I: Suggested standards for the medical examination of persons applying for or seeking renewal of driving licenses. Royal Automobile Club of Victoria, 123 Queen St., Melbourne, Vic. 3000, Australia.

13. Committee on Medicolegal Problems: Alcohol and the Impaired Driver. Chicago, American Medical Association, 1968.

14. Committee on Medical Aspects of Automotive Safety: Rating the severity of tissue damage. I. The abbreviated scale. JAMA 1971; 215:277-280. The revised (1985) edition is available from the American Association for Automotive Medicine, Arlington Heights, IL 60005.

Chapter 2

PHYSICIAN AND MOTOR VEHICLE ADMINISTRATOR

From the standpoint of society's well-being it is imperative to identify and keep records on those persons with impairments who wish to drive but who may pose a threat to themselves, to other drivers or to society at large. It also is important to identify already-licensed persons who have impairments.

To receive a license to drive, an impaired person first should be evaluated by a physician or by the state's medical review board. Thereafter, the person must successfully complete the driving examination of the state's motor vehicle agency. Many impaired persons will be safe drivers. It must be emphasized that, by law, the decision about licensing such persons and about restricting their driving rests with the state and not with the physician.

Because the physician may be involved in the licensing process by making a diagnosis and providing recommendations concerning a patient's condition, the relationship between the physician and the administrator of the state's driver-licensing agency is important. Especially desirable are an understanding of the respective responsibilities of the professions and forthright, respectful communications. Guidelines that the physician may use in providing competent medical evaluations appear in a recent AMA publication (1).

Physicians should understand that many referrals for medical evaluations will come from state licensing agencies. In many instances, well-trained driver's license examiners will have detected evidence of medical, physical or behavioral abnormalities that have prompted the referrals, or an agency may require re-examination of a particular driver. On the other hand, there may be special circumstances, as with patients having neurological or musculoskeletal impairments, when the physician may wish to ask the examiner to test the patient's ability to drive.

Physicians may become involved with state licensing agencies and motor vehicle administrators in other ways: state laws may require physicians to report persons with specific medical conditions; the physician may feel compelled to report a person whose medical condition may impair his or her driving; the licensing agency may ask the physician to provide information about a patient's condition, in which case it usually provides a signed form permitting release of the information; or the administrator may ask the physician to serve on the state's medical advisory board.

Driver's license examiners and administrators of licensing agencies have the responsibility of becoming familiar with medical conditions and impairments that can impair or limit people's driving ability. In this endeavor they would do well to develop good working relationships with those physicians who can discuss knowledgeably the impairments and disabilities of drivers and driver applicants.

Examiners should develop working relationships with physicians. Good relationships with state and county medical societies and with medical specialty societies also will be helpful. For instance, the administrator or examiner could help physicians by describing the philosophy of the licensing agency at a medical meeting or by contributing an article to the state's medical journal explaining the agency's functions and responsibilities.

Modern studies of injuries utilize epidemiologic methods similar to those established for the control of communicable diseases, which are useful in analyzing interrelationships among driver, vehicle, environment and other factors involved in crashes. Such studies are beginning to provide some guidance in licensing decisions. Local or state health departments may have staff members who are working on the problem of injuries and crashes; they would be ideal advisors and natural allies of examiners and licensing agency administrators.

Physicians are potential sources of information about drivers. Although progress has been made in enlisting the cooperation of physicians, much medical information remains inaccessible to licensing agencies because it is privileged communication between patient and physician, and disseminating it involves not only the ethics of the patient-physician relationship but also the possibility of litigation (2). Yet eight states have passed legislation requiring physicians to report certain conditions that may affect driving ability, such as epilepsy, lapses of consciousness or other physical or mental impairments (3).

Medical advisory boards or committees are used by many states to assist their licensing agencies and are highly recommended. Since 1966, the establishment of such boards has been a federal highway safety standard. The boards usually are composed of 6 to 20 physicians, and they have three functions. These may be dealt with by the board as a whole, or separate boards or committees may serve the different functions: advisory, referring to assistance in the setting of medical standards; review, referring to review of medical reports and recommendations about individuals; and appeals, referring to appeals from decisions of the state licensing agency.

Depending on their specific functions and responsibilities and state laws, medical advisory boards may have non-physician members, in particular, some who are involved in rehabilitation or who are knowledgeable about handicapped persons and injuries. These members help provide a broader perspective.

The role of the medical advisory board is to make a determination about the severity of the applicant's medical impairment in terms of driving. While the board attempts to forecast the effect of the impairment on the applicant's ability to function capably and safely in the driving situation, the final decision about licensing remains with the licensing agency.

Frequently, physicians will provide advice to their patients or to family members about limiting the amount or type of patients' driving. In these instances, because of medicolegal considerations, physicians should provide the advice in writing. The physician should keep a copy of the advice, describing it in the patient's record and noting the fact that it was given in written form.

The American Association of Motor Vehicle Administrators (AAMVA), in cooperation with the AMA and the federal National Highway Traffic Safety Administration, has published a booklet designed to assist medical advisory boards. Single copies of the publication, entitled "The Role of Medical Advisory Boards in Driver Licensing," may be obtained free from the AAMVA, 1201 Connecticut Ave. NW, Washington, D.C. 20036.

References

1. American Medical Association (AMA): Guides to the Evaluation of Permanent Impairment (2nd ed). Chicago, American Medical Association, 1984.

2. Waller JA: Hunting the evasive solutions to medical impairment and highway crashes. J Chron Dis 1977;30:393-400.

3. National Highway Traffic Safety Administration, U.S. Department of Transportation: Driver Licensing Laws Annotated 1980. Washington, D.C., U.S. Government Printing Office, p. 121.

Chapter 3

VISION

Although good vision is essential to the safe operation of a motor vehicle, the level of a driver's visual acuity is not related precisely to the frequency of crashes. For example, the driver with visual acuity of 20/40 would not be expected to have twice as many crashes per 10,000 miles driven as the driver with visual acuity of 20/20.

As with other medical impairments, the allowable impairment of a driver's vision relates to the driver's responsibilities and to the risk engendered by the condition. A classification of drivers according to the vehicles they drive appears in Chapter 1.

Corrected central visual acuity of 20/40 is accepted in most states as a minimum standard for drivers. Under standards of the American National Standards Institute and the U.S. Department of Transportation, freeway traffic signs are lettered in such a way that they are visible to a driver with 20/40 visual acuity moving at authorized maximum speeds and under normal weather conditions. This provides the driver of average intelligence ample time to interpret the sign and sufficient distance to perform any necessary maneuver. However, many signs fall below these standards.

Central Visual Acuity

Central visual acuity should be assessed at a standard distance of 20 feet (6 meters) with optimal refractive correction. The assessments should exclude the use of extremely high power spectacle lenses in the range of $\pm$ 10 diopters (D), binoculars, telescopes or low-vision-aid spectacles or compound magnifying systems, because such lenses distort and reduce the visual fields of the wearer. In all instances, the driver's acuity should be demonstrated promptly.

It is recommended that drivers in Class I have central visual acuity of 20/25 or better in each eye with or without conventional spectacle correction. Spectacle correction of 10 D or more in either eye should be disqualifying. A driver may be tested with contact lenses if he or she can wear them all day.

Drivers in Class II should have central acuity of at least 20/40 in the better eye and at least 20/60 in the other eye, in both instances with or without conventional spectacles or contact lenses. Spectacle correction of 10 D or more in either eye should be disqualifying unless waived by the examining physician on the basis of long-standing, functional adaptation.

It is recommended that drivers in Class III have central acuity of 20/40 or better in one eye or with both eyes open. Spectacle correction of 10 D or more in the better eye or in only one eye should be disqualifying unless a horizontal field of vision of 140° can be demonstrated.

Field of Vision

Impairment of visual fields is related to crashes at intersections involving the direction in which the driver has decreased peripheral vision (1). Total loss of visual field in one eye and monocular blindness also have been related to crashes (2,3). The Goldmann 30 cm radius bowl perimeter has become the reference standard for testing visual fields since its introduction in 1945. However, less cumbersome and less expensive equipment may be used.

The patient may not be aware of losses in peripheral fields. In testing fields of vision, the examiner may use confrontation testing with eye-to-eye fixation by examiner and examinee. The examiner measures awareness of a cotton-tip applicator or a moving finger at the periphery and compares it with his or her own visual fields, which must be normal.

Alternate methods of testing utilize the American Automobile Association's table model field-of-vision tester, which is 20 inches in diameter and encompasses approximately 220° horizontally; the Titmus push-button perimeter arc, adapted to the top surface of a Titmus vision tester; the simple hand-held Schweigger and Spiller rotating arc perimeters; and the hand-held C Perimeter (Figure). For screening purposes, the testing is confined to the horizontal arc and utilizes a 3 mm white target against a 330 mm radius arc or a Goldmann perimeter using the III 4e target.

For Class I drivers, each eye is tested separately while the other eye is obscured by an opaque occluder, preferably one that is tied around the head. The patient's spectacles or contact lenses should be worn during the visual field examination. Each eye should have visual field recognition throughout an arc of 140° or more. Individuals wearing spectacles with lenses exceeding 10 D or utilizing heavy spectacle frames generally cannot meet this standard.

Requirements for Class II drivers are the same as for Class I.

For Class III drivers, the test described above may be performed with both eyes open. The candidate should recognize the target throughout an arc of 140°.

Color Vision

The completely color blind or achromatic individual usually has poor central visual acuity and also may have visual field loss. The widespread modification of adding yellow to red and adding blue to green traffic signals has reduced the problem of red-green visual confusion, even in persons with significant deficiencies of red or green sensitivity.

Class I drivers should be able to distinguish the basic traffic control colors, red, green and amber, with each eye separately.

Class II requirements are the same as with Class I, but the patient may have both eyes open.

Class III drivers need not be tested for color discrimination.

Stereopsis

Stereopsis is almost exclusively a function of near vision, and it is tested by near-range equipment, such as a Verhoeff stereopter, the Wirt-Titmus double-printed polaroid vectograms, or random dot stereograms. Distance depth perception in driving does not relate to near range stereopsis, and it can be satisfactorily tested only with a road

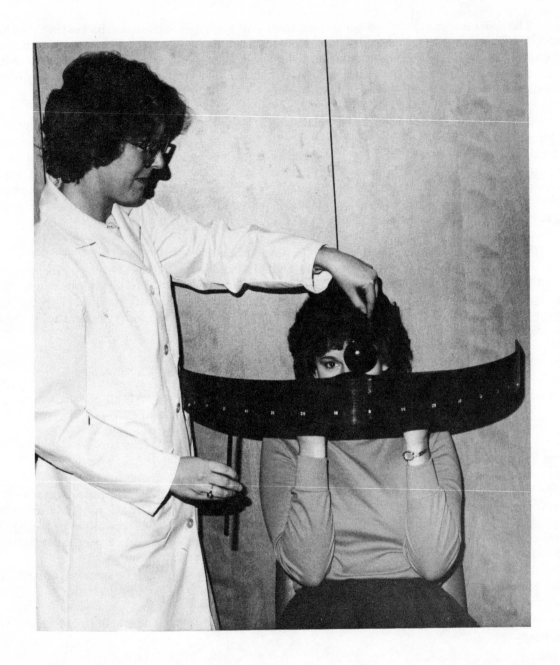

driving test. Testing of this function is not required to determine a driver's medical qualifications.

Nighttime Vision

Nighttime or mesopic visual functions are especially important because more crashes and more crashes with fatalities occur at night than during daytime hours (4). These functions generally are classified as (1) night vision or central acuity under reduced illumination; (2) glare tolerance or central acuity against a standardized glare light source; and (3) glare recovery time, as expressed in seconds necessary to regain satisfactory night vision after exposure to disabling glare. Economical and reliable testing procedures are not generally available, and results often are not reproducible (5).

For all three classes of drivers, therefore, the physician testing nighttime vision should attempt to detect morphologic and structural alterations of the eye that are known to affect it and its mesopic functions, such as corneal opacities; dystrophies or scars affecting the pupillary portion of the cornea; lens opacities, particularly those involving the pupillary or central portion of the lens; pigmentary degeneration of the retina; optic atrophy; degeneration of the maculae; or significant arteriosclerotic, diabetic or hypertensive retinopathy.

Diplopia and Oscillopsia

Binocular vision and fusion are the product of highly specialized and precise neurological functions. Factors known to impair these functions are alcohol ingestion, hypoxia and fatigue. Individuals vary greatly in their fusional capacities and in their tolerance of the impairing factors. A driver who develops diplopia soon will learn to close an eye to suppress one of the images. The occurrence of diplopia is relatively rare, but its presence could interfere with the safe operation of a motor vehicle.

Among the many neurological diseases that may produce diplopia is multiple sclerosis, and a high proportion of patients with that condition have nystagmus of a rapid, jerky type that may cause some blurring of the visual image. Gaze palsies of supranuclear origin and conditions involving the extraocular muscles or sixth cranial nerve also can cause diplopia. Ptosis due to a condition affecting the third nerve may reduce the visual field. Acute optic neuritis reduces vision on the side of the affected nerve; symptoms may clear in days or weeks but recurrences are frequent.

Drivers presenting signs or symptoms of impaired fusion usually are medically qualified to receive Class III licenses. To be medically qualified for a Class I or a Class II license, the driver should have a waiver from the examining physician based on long-standing functional adaptation.

Transient States Affecting Vision

Transient obscuring of vision may accompany an altered physiologic state, as with elevation or depression of the blood sugar level. A change in vision also may occur when the physician dilates the patient's pupils as part of a medical examination. The mydriasis may be brief, as with the use of short-acting drugs, or may last a few days, as with the use of atropine and long-acting drugs.

When the pupils are dilated, the patient may be troubled by glare and have difficulty with near-focusing. The physician should advise about the possibility of such problems. The patient may use dark glasses to increase comfort after the examination, avoid driving and adjust his or her activities according to the duration of the symptoms.

The patient who must have a dressing placed over one eye will be without the usual stereopsis, and the limited visual field will increase the risk of misadventure and injury. It is recommended that the patient not drive under these circumstances. Suddenly occurring monocularity is more incapacitating then monocularity that has been present for a long period of time (6).

While pilocarpine has been useful for more than a century in the medical control of glaucoma, it causes miosis and myopia. Thus, using this drug may interfere with night driving and with visual cues for distance. The patient should be informed of these effects.

The use of soft lens materials and of extended-wear contact lenses has increased greatly in recent years. Physical activities, wind currents and the general environment associated with driving may cause visual disturbances in persons who wear these lenses, and the disturbances increase as the dioptric power of the lenses increases. Dislocation of the lens may occur with sudden turning of the head, or there may be induced diplopia because of movement of the lens over the cornea.

Soft and extended-wear lenses, which may contan 30% to 75% water, are subject to dehydration from air currents, which may lead to visual blurring. Correcting this condition usually requires a series of blinks, during which time a driver might be incapacitated. Persons who are starting to wear these lenses should be advised to avoid the drafts of air conditioners, open windows and convertible automobiles that may lead to visual disturbances (7).

References

1. Freytag E, Sachs JC: Abnormalities of the central visual pathways contributing to Maryland traffic accidents. JAMA 1968; 204:119-121.

2. Keeney AH, Garvey JL, Brunker JA: Current experience with the monocular driver in Kentucky. Proc Amer Assoc Auto Med 1981; pp 215-220.

3. Kite CR, King JN: A survey of the factors limiting the visual fields of motor vehicle drivers in relation to minimum visual fields and visibility standards. Br J Physiol Opt 1961; 18:85.

4. Statistics Department, National Safety Council (NSC): Accident Facts 1984 Edition. Chicago, NSC, 1984 p. 50.

5. Henderson RL, Burg A: Driver screening for night driving. Chapter in "Driver Visual Needs in Night Driving" (Special Report 156). Washington, D.C., Transportation Research Board of the National Academy of Sciences, 1975, pp 74-89.

6. Brady FB: A Singular View: The Art of Seeing With One Eye. Oradell, New Jersey, Medical Economics Company, 1972.

7. Keeney AH, Shrader EC: Kinetic visual disturbances with contact lenses. Survey of Ophth 1983; 28:112-116.

Chapter 4

HEARING

Conditions involving impaired hearing that can affect a person's ability to operate a motor vehicle may be classified into three categories: those affecting auditory sensitivity or hearing acuity; those altering communicative ability or hearing perception related to speech; and those limiting motor ability because of dizziness, vertigo or labyrinthitis. A medical condition can involve more than one of these functions at the same time (1).

Hearing Deficiencies

Severe hearing loss or deafness is a handicap to driving, but the relationship between hearing loss and ability to operate a motor vehicle safely is difficult to define. Hearing also can be affected by a loudly playing radio or tape deck, and auditory cues from the outside tend to be eliminated by the sound conditioning of the modern automobile's passenger compartment.

Research studies involving deaf and hard-of-hearing drivers are not in complete agreement, but they tend to indicate that the deaf are safe drivers. Booher's summary (2) of current studies shows a better-than-average driving record for the hearing-impaired. An exception is one study that compared two large populations of deaf and nondeaf drivers with regard to a number of variables (3). Although deaf females did not differ from nondeaf females in either the number of accumulated violation points or crashes, deaf males from urban areas had a crash rate 1.8 times higher than that of nondeaf males from urban areas.

A related factor may be age. Roydhouse (4) surveyed 220 deaf and hard-of-hearing drivers in New Zealand and found that the drivers less than 50 years old had a crash rate lower than the national average, and those over 50 had a crash rate higher than the average.

Auditory Requirements for Driving

Few conclusions are possible about the specific auditory requirements necessary for safe driving. One critical task, listening for train whistles and horns at grade crossings, was found to be a unique auditory requirement for safe driving (5). Other requirements appear to be less clear and more speculative. In one study, deleting auditory cues simulating engine noise appeared to decrease safe driving responses (6). Yet there is evidence that increased ambient noise in a moving vehicle decreases the safety values of auditory cues by interfering with warning signals.

It is generally accepted by licensing officials that deaf or hard-of-hearing persons can compensate for their handicaps sufficiently well with increased visual vigilance to drive private vehicles and light commercial trucks safely (2,7,8). However, the drivers of larger commercial vehicles should be able to hear above the noise of engines, especially in cities and congested areas, and drivers of passenger-carrying or emergency vehicles should be able to hear well enough to communicate adequately with their riders (1).

Considerable variability exists among the states with regard to defining the criteria for allowable hearing loss and restricting the hearing-impaired driver (3). A questionnaire that physicians may find useful when evaluating an applicant's hearing function related to speech is shown in Table 1. It is adapted from one developed by Roydhouse (4), who found that questionnaire responses and results from speech audiometry compared favorably.

Recommendations

The guidelines in Table 2 are based on the evaluation of monaural hearing impairment as described in an AMA publication (9). The evaluation incorporates pure tone audiometry and the use of four frequencies to determine hearing level, 500, 1000, 2000 and 3000 Herz. The 40 dB cutoff level for monaural hearing impairment (22.5% impairment) is based upon the general observation by physicians and audiologists that amplification with a hearing aid is usually needed when the estimated hearing level for speech exceeds 35 dB (10).

Tests with speech may be used to corroborate the average hearing threshold levels for pure tones in each ear. It is recommended that use of a hearing aid be permitted only for drivers in Class III. Drivers with hearing that is impaired according to the guidelines in Table 2 should have good vision, that is, they should be able to meet the visual standards for drivers in Class II. It is recommended that a review of each impaired driver's hearing and medical status take place at intervals of two to three years.

Equilibrium

Impairments of equilibrium occur in any disorder causing vertigo or disorientation in space. A classification of impairments of equilibrium secondary to vestibular disorders is presented in the AMA publication on permanent impairment (9). Any disorder affecting the nervous or vestibular system and resulting in disorientation, impaired sense of balance or vertigo should disqualify a driver from operating a vehicle until the condition has been controlled completely. This disqualification would apply to most individuals in impairment Class 2 and to all individuals in impairment Classes 3 through 5, as those classes are defined in the AMA publication (9).

A questionnaire that physicians may find useful when evaluating applicants with a history of balance or vestibular disorder is shown in Table 3.

Other Factors

Special modifications of drivers' training courses for hearing-impaired students, with appropriate graphics and captions, have been found to be more effective than traditional training methods (11). Drivers and hearing-impaired patients should be reminded that pedestrians with hearing impairments are at greater risk of injury by automobiles, especially if they are elderly, than are persons with normal hearing (12).

Drivers should not wear earphones because they will interfere with ambient sounds. Several states have passed legislation prohibiting this practice. The specific effects on a driver's performance of using earphones, a telephone or a loud audio system and the effect on a pedestrian of wearing earphones need to be investigated.

17

Table 1

Hearing Questionnaire *

<u>Instructions</u>: Please circle the correct answer.

(1) Do you have a hearing loss?   Yes   No

(2) If "yes," in which ear?   Right   Left   Both

How good is your hearing?

(3) Is it difficult to hear at lectures, meetings,
     church?   Yes   No

(4) Is it difficult to hear general conversation?   Yes   No

(5) Is it difficult to hear the speaking of a
     person close to you?   Yes   No

(6) Can you hear the speaking of a person close
     to you only when his or her voice is raised?   Yes   No

(7) Do you wear a hearing aid?   Yes   No

(8) Can you understand speech with the hearing aid?   Yes   No

* Adapted from ref. 4.

18

Table 2

Recommendations for Licensing Drivers with Hearing Defects

Class of Driver*	Hearing Loss Characteristics	Recommendations
I	Average hearing threshold level** in better ear is less than 40 dB by pure tone air conduction audiometry and more than 40 dB in poorer ear. In testing, correction by hearing aid is not recommended.	These drivers should not drive passenger-carrying vehicles.
II	Average hearing threshold level** is more than 40 dB by pure tone air conduction audiometry in each ear. In testing, correction by hearing aid is not recommended.	These drivers should not drive heavy commercial transport vehicles.
III	Average hearing threshold level** is more than 40 dB by pure tone air conduction audiometry in the better ear, with or without hearing aid correction.	Two sideview mirrors and an internal rearview mirror, and successful completion of a special course for deaf drivers are recommended. Daytime driving only is recommended.
	Average hearing threshold level** is less than 40 dB in the better ear and more than 40 dB in the poorer ear with or without hearing aid correction.	There are no restrictions, but two sideview mirrors are recommended.

*   Classes of drivers are described in Chapter 1.

** Average hearing threshold level is the simple average of pure tone
    air conduction thresholds for each ear at 500, 1000, 2000 and 3000
    Hz (10).

Table 3

Equilibrium Questionnaire

<u>Instructions</u>: Please circle the correct answer.

(1) Within the past two years have you had any problems
     with balance, walking, dizziness or vertigo?   Yes   No

(2) Do you become dizzy when lying down or turning
     in bed?   Yes   No

(3) Do you lose consciousness at times?   Yes   No

(4) Are you under a physician's care for dizziness
     or for a balance problem?   Yes   No

(5) Can you walk in the dark without assistance?   Yes   No

(6) Are you taking any medication for dizziness?   Yes   No

References

1.   National Highway Traffic Safety Administration, U.S. Department of Transportation: Functional Aspects of Driver Impairment, A Guide for State Medical Advisory Boards. Washington, D.C., U.S. Government Printing Office, 1980.

2.   Booher HR: Effects of visual and auditory impairment in driving performance. Human Factors 1978; 20:307-320.

3.   Coppin RS, Peck RC: The totally deaf driver in California Part I. California Department of Motor Vehicles, Division of Administration, Report No. 16, December, 1964.

4.   Roydhouse N: Deafness and driving. New Zealand Med J 1967; 66:878-881.

5.   Henderson RL, Burg A: Vision and audition in driving. Santa Monica, CA, System Development Corp, 1974, cited in Booher (2).

6.   McLane RC, Wierwille WW: The influence of motion and audio cues on drivers' performance in an automobile simulator. Human Factors 1975; 17:488-501.

7.   Ysander L: Sick and handicapped drivers. Acta Chir Scand 1970; Suppl 409, chapter III, pages 15-16, and Appendix II, pages 77-78.

8.   Waller JA: Medical Impairments to Driving.   Springfield, IL, Charles C. Thomas, 1973.

9.   Ear, nose, throat and related structures.   Chapter 7 in American Medical Association: Guides to the Evaluation of Permanent Impairment (2nd Edition). Chicago, American Medical Association, 1984.

10.   Martin FN: Introduction to Audiology. Chapter 12, Audiological Management of the Patient. Englewood Cliffs, NJ, Prentice-Hall, 1975.

11.   Sendelbaugh JW: Driver simulator communication mode for hearing-impaired students. Amer Ann Deaf 1980;125:542-546.

12.   Grattan E, Jeffcoate GO: Medical factors in road accidents.   Brit Med J 1968; 1:75-79.

Chapter 5

DIABETES MELLITUS AND OTHER ENDOCRINE DISORDERS

Diabetes Mellitus

Decisions about placing limitations on the driving of persons with diabetes mellitus depend on four factors that are similar to those relating to job placement of the diabetic patient: status of medical supervision and self-care (compliance), type of treatment, status of metabolic control, and presence of complications (1).

Status of Medical Supervision and Self-Care

Assessing the effect of diabetes on driving ability requires knowledge of the patient's metabolic control during the past several months or years and especially about the occurrence of severe or frequent episodes of hypoglycemic coma. Usually the degree of control cannot be determined unless the individual has been under continuing medical care. It is possible that the person applying for a driver's license will not give an accurate history. Therefore, it is recommended that a physician not certify a diabetic individual as being medically qualified to drive unless the individual has been his or her regular patient.

When the diabetic individual visits a physician for the first time, for instance, because of relocation, transfer from pediatrician to internist, death or retirement of the previous physician or desire to see a specialist, the new physician should obtain and examine previous medical records before certifying that the individual is medically able to drive.

A diabetic patient's condition may change significantly over time, which makes necessary periodic evaluation of the patient's state of metabolic control. Persons who are unreliable in keeping appointments or who do not have periodic examinations may be at increased risk of deteriorating metabolic control. On the other hand, a person who shows a good understanding of the condition and how it can affect driving ability may be treated more liberally by the physician and by the medical advisory board (2). For instance, the person who understands and follows a proper diet, does frequent blood or urine glucose measurements at home and takes prescribed medication would be less likely to have an undetected change in control and would require less frequent examination and evaluation.

In Illinois, the chief licensing official may require an applicant having a medical condition that may affect safe driving to sign an agreement to remain under the physician's care, follow the prescribed treatment and notify the official upon changing physicians. The agreement authorizes the physician to report any change in the condition that might affect safe driving. Such agreements may help assure the physician's continuing care and the patient's compliance with therapy.

Type of Treatment

Of greatest significance to the safe driving of diabetic patients are alterations of consciousness (2). While persons with diabetes under any kind of treatment may develop <u>hyperglycemic</u> states that impair alertness, including diabetic ketoacidosis and

22

hyperosmolar syndromes, these states usually are of gradual onset. The person who understands the symptoms of hyperglycemia and who does frequent self-monitoring is not likely to drive in such situations.

Much more dangerous is hypoglycemia, which may occur suddenly and without warning. Hypoglycemia is most common in insulin-treated persons, but it also can occur as a reaction to oral hypoglycemic agents. Hypoglycemia is infrequent in the diabetic person treated only with diet.

Persons whose diabetes is controlled with diet only may drive any type of motor vehicle if they otherwise meet the medical standards. Individuals with a history of diabetes in the past but who presently require no insulin or other treatment also may drive any type of vehicle. The latter group includes persons with histories of gestational, stress-induced or steroid-induced diabetes. A history of taking insulin in the past for these transient situations should not disqualify a person from driving any type of vehicle if there is no present evidence of diabetes.

The condition of impaired glucose tolerance, which is defined as a fasting blood glucose level below 140 mg/dl and a two-hour value in a standard glucose tolerance test between 140 and 200 mg/dl, generally does not require treatment except for possible modification of the diet, and this condition need not restrict driving.

Diabetics who take insulin or oral hypoglycemic agents and whose blood glucose control is unstable should be evaluated individually as described under the section below on metabolic control. Both the physician and the diabetic patient should understand that federal regulations prohibit the driving of vehicles involved in interstate or foreign commerce by persons taking insulin (2).

Status of Metabolic Control

Because the possibility of loss of consciousness is the most important consideration in evaluating whether a person can operate a motor vehicle safely, physicians evaluating diabetic individuals should classify them in one of three groups as follows (2):

Medical group A - The individual has not had an episode of altered consciousness due to diabetes mellitus during the preceding three years and is not taking medication, including insulin.

Medical group B - The individual has not had an episode of altered consciousness due to diabetes mellitus for one year, either while using or while not using medication.

Medical group C - The individual has had an episode of altered consciousness in the preceding year due to diabetes mellitus, either while using or while not using medication.

In terms of the above classification, the U.S. Department of Transportation (2) recommends that persons be approved for driving various vehicles according to the specifications in Table 1.

The U.S. Department of Transportation recommends a "restricted" license for persons subject to "stress hypoglycemia" (2), but because this condition cannot be defined

23

Table 1

Recommendations Pertaining to Metabolic Control
and Loss of Consciousness

Medical Group*	Recommended Class** of Driver			Other Recommendations		
	I	II	III	Periodic Re-evaluation	Unrestricted License	Restricted License
A	Yes	Yes	Yes	Yes	Yes	No
B	No	Yes	Yes	Yes	Yes	No
C	No	No	Yes	Yes	No	Yes

* See definitions on preceding pages.

** Classes of drivers' medical qualifications
   are defined in Chapter 1.

easily, the physician may wish to consider the recommendations of the Utah Department of Public Safety (3) for persons in Medical group C:

1. Persons with stabilized diabetes and with no episodes of ketoacidosis or altered consciousness during the preceding six months may have unlimited use of private vehicles.

2. Persons with stabilized diabetes and with no episodes of ketosis or altered consciousness during the preceding three months may be restricted with regard to speed and be re-evaluated in six months.

3. Persons with episodes of ketosis or with altered consciousness within three months of examination may be restricted with regard to speed, area of driving and time of day when they may drive, and may need to be accompanied by a licensed driver.

4. Persons with severe, unstable, insulin-dependent diabetes or persisting ketosis should not drive.

In some instances, state licensing agencies may mandate restrictions such as those listed above, but in other instances they may not require such restrictions. The physician, nonetheless, may wish to use the Utah recommendations, in which case the restrictions should be noted in the patient's record.

Depending on state laws, a person with adult-onset (type II) diabetes who is stable on low doses of insulin may be allowed to drive passenger buses, heavy trucks and emergency vehicles within that state, if this is recommended by the physician and approved by the medical advisory board (3). According to federal law, however, such a person should not drive those types of vehicles in interstate or foreign commerce.

Persons with episodic hyperglycemia may have transient blurring of vision. The individual is usually aware of this and should not drive during these periods.

Complications of Diabetes

Diabetes may affect vision, the cardiovascular system and the nervous system. Persons with such impairments should be evaluated using the specific recommendations given in other chapters of this publication.

Some individuals with diabetic autonomic neuropathy lose their ability to recognize hypoglycemia. A patient with this condition usually is identified when he or she gives a history of no longer developing the usual warning symptoms of insulin reactions (4). In such a situation driving may be extremely hazardous. These patients should not be permitted to drive unless blood (not urine) glucose levels are tested before driving and periodically during long drives (about every two hours) and found to be in an acceptable range. The same precautions should be taken for persons using insulin and being treated with beta-adrenergic blocking agents, which also can interfere with the recognition of hypoglycemia.

Other Metabolic and Endocrine Disorders

Most endocrine and metabolic disorders can be treated satisfactorily once the initial diagnosis is made. In contrast to the situation with some diabetic patients, limitations on driving are not necessary. The recommendations of the Utah Medical Advisory Board (3) may be used (Table 2). If the suggested restrictions are not mandated by the state's licensing agency, the physician nevertheless may wish to suggest them to the patient, in which case the recommendations should be noted in the patient's record.

A patient with a pituitary tumor may develop visual field defects, particularly in the temporal fields, but may be unaware of the impaired vision (5). The resulting loss of lateral vision may be the cause of automobile crashes. The field defects may not reverse after treatment and may increase if the tumor grows or recurs. Tests of the visual fields should be performed every 6 to 12 months until they are stable.

Persons with pituitary insufficiency, if not adequately treated, may have hypoglycemic episodes. They should be evaluated in a manner similar to diabetic patients.

Acutely thyrotoxic or severely hypothyroid persons should not drive. Because such patients frequently are hospitalized or confined to their homes, recommendations about their driving rarely are needed.

Extremely high or low calcium levels, as in persons with disorders of the parathyroid gland, may lead to muscular weakness, muscle spasms, or confusion or other alterations of consciousness. Patients with unstable serum calcium levels should not be permitted to drive. When the calcium level is stable, with or without therapy, there is no need to restrict driving.

Persons with adrenal cortical hyperfunction (Cushing's syndrome) should not drive if they have severe muscle weakness. Persons with adrenal insufficiency (Addison's disease) should not drive if they are subject to hypoglycemia or syncope. When the condition is stable and adrenal hormone replacement treatment is instituted, they may meet the medical qualifications in Class III.

Patients with disorders of hypoglycemia should be evaluated in the same way as diabetic patients. Their abilities to function will depend on the etiology of the hypoglycemic symptoms and the response to treatment.

Table 2

Guidelines Concerning Metabolic Disorders

Status of Patient and Disorder	Suggested Class* of Medical Qualifications	Suggested Review Interval
No history of metabolic disorder.		normal
Abnormal laboratory findings, no diagnosis made.	Class I	normal
Stabliized under treatment, or recovered after surgery and without symptoms for one month.		1 year**
Stabilized under treatment and with minimal symptoms not affecting driving.	Class II	1 year**
Stabilized under treatment with minimal or slight, persisting or intermittent symptoms. The physician may recommend that one of the three restrictions listed in the middle column be placed on the driver. The recommendation should be based on the anticipated effect of the condition on driving.	Class III without restrictions, or with speed limitation, or with speed and area limitations, or with speed, area and time-of-day limitations.	1 year** 6 months** 6 months** 6 months**
Stabilized condition but with unpredictable and temporary recurrence of more severe symptoms.	Class III, with any of the above restrictions, providing the patient is accompanied by a licensed driver.	6 months**
Severe disorder not responsive to treatment.	None	

*Definitions of classes are listed in Chapter 1.

**The interval may be changed by the physician according to stability of the condition.

References

1. Friedman GJ: Employment and insurability. Chapter 11 in Schnatz JD (ed), Diabetes Mellitus: Problems in Management. Addison-Wesley, Menlo Park, CA 1982, pp 135-149.

2. National Highway Traffic Safety Administration, U.S. Department of Transportation: Functional Aspects of Driver Impairment - A Guide for State Medical Advisory Boards. Washington, D.C., U.S. Government Printing Office, 1980, pp 24-25.

3. Utah State Driver License Medical Advisory Board: Functional Ability in Driving: Guidelines for Physicians. Salt Lake City, Utah Department of Public Safety, 1981.

4. Haunz EA, Brosseau JD: Nonwarning hypoglycemia in drivers with diabetes. Amer Fam Physician 1984; 30:189-197.

5. Christy NP: Diagnosis and treatment of pituitary tumors. In Wyngaarden JB, Smith LH (eds): Cecil Textbook of Medicine (16th ed). Philadelphia, WB Saunders, 1982, pp 1179-1180.

Chapter 6

NEUROLOGICAL DISORDERS

Recommendations about limiting a patient's driving because of a neurological disorder should be based on the patient's neurological functioning rather than on a diagnostic term per se. For instance, those responsible for licensing drivers might allow a patient with epilepsy to drive and not allow one with the usually benign condition of migraine to drive, if the patient with epilepsy had only slight functional impairment and the person with migraine were significantly impaired.

Neurological dysfunctions vary considerably in type and degree (1,2). The aim of this chapter is to present general guidelines that will help physicians recognize and evaluate such dysfunctions. In most instances the evaluations may be based on the history, physical examination and neurological examination, but laboratory procedures may be indicated.

In this chapter, neurological dysfunctions are divided into four broad categories: alterations of the state of consciousness; disturbances of motor and coordinative ability; disturbances of sensory functions; and disturbances of higher cerebral functions.

Alterations of the State of Consciousness

Epilepsy constitutes an important problem with regard to driving an automobile. The existence of any type of epileptiform or seizure disorder without any of the mitigating circumstances described below must lead to the immediate and complete withdrawal of the privilege of driving a motor vehicle.

Epilepsy comes in many guises, which range from the dramatic grand mal seizure to the subtle psychomotor, temporal lobe or petit mal seizure that may be difficult to recognize (3). The diagnosis of epilepsy is a clinical one that is often but not always confirmed by the presence of an abnormal electroencephalogram (EEG). It should be emphasized that the presence of an abnormal EEG in a patient who never has had epileptiform seizures does not prove the diagnosis of epilepsy or constitute an indication for denying driving privileges. Conversely, the absence of EEG abnormalities is not proof that the patient does not have epilepsy. A neurologist's opinion may be helpful in determining whether a patient has epilepsy.

Because of the importance of driving in our society and the recognition that the diagnosis of epilepsy often affects the matter of driving privileges, many patients with epilepsy will attempt to disguise the nature of their disease. The physician should understand that although a patient may admit having seizures or "fainting spells," he or she may vigorously deny having "epilepsy."

Epileptiform seizures do not always cause loss of consciousness, but they often lead to an alteration in the state of consciousness (3). For instance, temporal lobe epilepsy may be indicated by or associated with distortions of visual and auditory experiences, confusion, disorientation and bizarre behavior. Simple dizziness or slight clouding of consciousness or thought processes may constitute the only manifestation. In such an instance the EEG may be helpful in making the diagnosis. Petit mal seizures may be of such short duration that neither the patient nor an observer may be aware of them, but they may be particularly dangerous in the automobile driver.

A patient with epilepsy may have an aura, that is, a sensation that precedes or heralds a seizure. The patient may state that there is enough time between the aura and the onset of the seizure to allow him to drive the car to the side of the road and stop. While this may be true in some instances, auras have no regular pattern of occurrence and should not be depended upon to reduce drivers' risks.

Special consideration must be given to patients who have seizures only during sleep and to those who have had an isolated seizure because of sleep deprivation. If a second seizure were to occur, even as the result of prolonged sleep deprivation, the patient would be considered to have epilepsy and would be subject to the same recommendations as persons with epilepsy.

Persons with epilepsy must be warned against driving when unduly fatigued, especially if they have not had their usual amounts of sleep, because sleep deprivation is one of the most common triggers of seizures. Individuals who have demonstrable sensitivity to stimulation by intermittent light should not drive at night, because the light (photic) stimuli from oncoming cars or roadside reflectors may induce seizures.

The physician should monitor carefully the effects of anticonvulsant medication on a patient's state of consciousness. Classes of drugs that can alter consciousness and affect driving skills are listed in Chapter 12 (Table 2).

In most states, epilepsy is not a reportable disease and the patient is free to follow the physician's advice or not (4). The physician should give a written copy of any recommendations to the patient and keep a copy in the chart.

Narcolepsy, the unheralded occurrence of sleep, poses a major threat to the driver (5). This form of hypersomnia usually is recognized by the inappropriate circumstances in which the patient may fall asleep, for example, in the middle of a meal. The condition usually responds well to medication. Forms of hypersomnia, such as the Pickwickian syndrome, sleep apnea and nonspecific hypersomnia, should be handled like narcolepsy. Any suspicion of a sleep disorder that might cause a risk during driving should receive thorough investigation by a qualified specialist or sleep clinic, and recommendations should be based on the findings.

The following recommendations concerning alterations of consciousness are made:

The presence of an abnormal EEG without a history of seizures should not by itself cause the withdrawal or withholding of licensing.

No patient having epilepsy or narcolepsy should be considered to be medically qualified in the Class I or Class II categories.

A patient with epilepsy may receive medical qualification in Class III if the conditions in one of the following categories are fulfilled.

1. The patient is receiving medication and is known to be taking it, and the medication has no side effects that might hamper driving ability; and the patient is under the care of a neurologist or other physician with training and expertise in neurology and has been seizure-free for at least 12 months.

Licensing after a seizure-free period of only six months may be considered under the following circumstances: the patient had no more than four seizures while not receiving anticonvulsant medication during the 12 months preceding the six-months' seizure-free period on medication.

2. The patient has a history of epilepsy but is not taking medication for seizures and has been seizure-free for at least 24 months according to the examination of a neurologist or other physician with expertise in neurology.

3. The patient has only nocturnal seizures and has been followed by a neurologist or other physician with training and competence in neurology for at least two years, or the patient has had only one sleep-deprivation seizure.

A patient with narcolepsy may be medically qualified in Class III if he or she has been symptom-free for at least six months and is taking medication.

Disturbances of Motor and Coordinative Functions

Normal strength is needed for patients to manipulate the steering wheel, the gear shift and the brake and accelerator pedals. Paralysis of the lower extremities usually can be compensated by installation of hand controls in the car. Any conditions leading to weakness of one or more of the extremities should limit the patient's driving until appropriate recovery has occurred or the necessary accessory equipment has been installed. A patient having impairment of the right or left foot or leg may be qualified medically in Class III if the vehicle involved has automatic transmission.

Weakness of the extremities is especially likely to occur in patients with strokes, multiple sclerosis and related diseases, peripheral neuropathies, various of diseases of the musculoskeletal system, trauma, neoplasms of the brain or spinal cord, osteoarthritis involving the cervical or lumbosacral vertebrae, or degenerative disc diseases (6,7). Rehabilitative efforts can diminish such weakness and improve capabilities. (See also Chapter 10.)

The more insidious, intermittent weakness and double vision that are manifestations of myasthenia gravis also must be recognized and controlled with appropriate medication.

Parkinsonism is a problem that deserves special attention. While many persons with that condition do not manifest sufficient motor weakness to warrant limiting their driving, their slowness of movement and rigidity greatly prolong reaction times. As a result, these persons are unable to respond as quickly as necessary to changing conditions. On that basis alone, their driving should be discouraged until they can demonstrate improvement, for instance, after receiving appropriate medication. Re-examination by a neurologist or other physician with neurological training and expertise is recommended, with particular attention to the reaction time. A test of driving capability may be helpful.

A rare condition is the myotonia seen with a special form of dystrophy and occasionally encountered in other conditions, such as amyotrophic lateral sclerosis. The patient with myotonia is unable to relax contracted muscles quickly. After prolonged sitting in a fixed position, the patient may find it difficult to move, to relax the hand clenched around the steering wheel or to move the foot quickly from gas pedal to brake.

Involuntary motor movements can interfere with the operation of the vehicle. A sudden, unexpected and occasionally strong movement of the arms and legs, as seen in the various forms of chorea and occasionally with severe myoclonus, may have disastrous results when translated into an unexpected motion of the steering wheel or a sudden depression of the accelerator. The uncontrolled movements of dystonia may have similar but slower effects (8).

The ability to act correctly, coordinate various movements and smoothly release the antagonistic muscles when the agonists are being contracted is essential to the proper operation of the vehicle, especially in steering, operating the gear shift, braking and accelerating (8,9). Any interference with the patient's coordination resulting from involvement of the cerebellum and its associated structures should limit driving. Conditions in which such problems occur include the spinocerebellar degenerations, multiple sclerosis, vascular diseases of the cerebellum and strokes involving the vertebral basilar system.

It is recommended that a patient with one of the conditions described above that is ongoing and progressive be considered only for qualification in Class III until a neurologist or other physician with training and expertise in neurology certifies that the person is capable of safely carrying out greater driving responsibilities.

Any condition that causes muscle weakness should be re-evaluated when it is stable; this should include evaluation by a physical or occupational therapist and the evaluation of driving skills with any needed prosthesis or adaptive device in place.

The patient with myasthenia gravis or myotonia who wishes to drive should be under the supervision of a neurologist or other physician with expertise in neurology, should be following recommended treatment, should not be taking drugs that have undesirable side effects that interfere with driving and should have been without symptoms for at least six months.

A patient with involuntary movements or one lacking motor coordination who wishes to drive should meet the standards given for individuals with myasthenia gravis, unless the condition is transitory, has stabilized and the guidelines for muscle weakness are met.

Disturbances of Sensory Functions

If double vision occurs, as with myasthenia gravis or multiple sclerosis, the question of whether the patient ought to drive may be resolved by a road test. A central scotoma would not disqualify the patient from driving if he were able to meet the standards for central visual acuity and peripheral vision. Other guidelines concerning vision and hearing appear in Chapters 3 and 4.

Position (muscle-, joint- and tendon-) sense is important in that it allows the driver to move the foot between brake and gas pedal or to shift gears without watching. Severe loss of position sense, which is common in diseases such as multiple sclerosis and the polyneuropathies, may be reason to recommend that an individual not drive. Loss of this sense usually affects the feet and legs and commonly is associated with weakness; installing hand controls may solve the problem. Pernicious anemia also may lead to this problem; fortunately, specific treatment is available.

Vertigo or dizziness, a subjective sensation related to the vestibular system, can be extremely disabling (10). Attacks usually occur suddenly and without warning and may cause the patient to lose control of the vehicle. Patients subject to such episodes should not drive until the condition has cleared up, either spontaneously or as a result of treatment, and they have been without symptoms for six months.

Certain types of pain are extremely severe, may occur suddenly without warning and may produce a shock that interferes with operation of the vehicle. Chief among them is the severe pain of trigeminal neuralgia (tic douloureux), in which extremely severe, sharp, needle-like jabs of pain occur in parts of the face. Similar conditions include atypical facial pain, glossopharyngeal neuralgia, temporomandibular joint syndrome, post-herpetic neuralgia and tabetic pains. Other forms of severe pain may be related to chronic lumbosacral sprain or herniated disc.

Migraine almost always is preceded by an aura or warning or by a slowly developing crescendo of headache pain, making it obvious that driving should not be undertaken (11). Cluster headaches, which may be related to fatigue or lack of sleep, may occur suddenly, be severe and disabling and interfere with driving. If they are controlled by medication, cluster headaches usually are not a contraindication to driving.

Driving privileges of patients with the conditions described above may be temporarily withdrawn and restored if the condition disappears. If the condition persists but has stabilized, specific evaluation by an occupational or physical therapist and evaluation of driving skills should be sought before making a recommendation about driving.

If severe loss of position sense persists, as in vitamin B_{12} deficiency and multiple sclerosis, adaptive devices for hand controls may be required and the driver can meet the medical qualifications of Class III only. With vertigo or dizziness, the recommendations outlined for epilepsy should be applied. In instances of severe episodic pain, such as trigeminal neuralgia, an interval of six months without pain is recommended before any type of driving is resumed.

Disturbances of Higher Cerebral Functions

Drivers must assimilate information and interpret cues continuously, making decisions based upon ever-changing interactions with other automobiles and drivers and the environment. Therefore, they should be of at least "normal" intelligence. Persons who are severely mentally handicapped probably will fail written drivers' tests, and the licensing of such persons would not be expected.

Those individuals who have been of normal intelligence but whose mental abilities have deteriorated because of dementing illnesses pose a serious problem. Early dementia, whatever its cause, is often difficult to recognize (12). The early signs of impaired recent memory are not expected to interfere with driving. It is not until later in the course of the disease, after some major error in handling the car has occurred, that the problem is called to the physician's attention. Once the presence of dementia is established and it is demonstrated that the patient is at risk of making errors of judgment likely to affect the ability to drive safely, an individual should not drive again.

Evidence concerning higher cerebral functions should be carefully sought in persons who have had strokes or have experienced cerebral trauma. The evidence might include language disturbances, such as alexia, with loss of the ability to read street names and traffic signs; auditory agnosia, with inability to understand spoken directions; alteration of the body image interfering with ability to maneuver the car, not only on the road but also in parking or in entering or leaving a garage; and inattention to or denial of space and of the body on the opposite side from the affected hemisphere (13).

The last-named condition, neglect, usually involves the left side of the body and may occur in a patient who has suffered a vascular, traumatic, or neoplastic lesion of the right hemisphere. Such patients are completely unaware of events, situations, objects or occurrences involving the left side of the body, even if there is no impairment of the left visual field. Patients who demonstrate the phenomenon of extinction after bilateral simultaneous stimulation may have what amounts to inattention to one side, a condition that invariably occurs while driving. The conditions described above are subtle ones that pose serious risks to the driver and the public. Often only a skilled neurologist is able to demonstrate them. Their discovery should lead to recommendations against driving and licensing.

Alterations of higher cerebral functions are rarely transient, except when they are part of a more general illness involving the nervous system, such as encephalitis, cerebrovascular accident or intoxication, which by itself would cause the patient to stop driving. Alterations of higher cerebral functions existing by themselves or persisting after the acute phase of brain disease should result in complete, permanent withdrawal of driving privileges. The only exception would be if it were conclusively shown by appropriate neurological and neuropsychological examinations that the alterations of higher cerebral function were due to depression that responded to medicinal or other forms of treatment. Under such circumstances, driving privileges according to Class III medical qualifications might be recommended after close observation by a neurologist or a psychiatrist for a period of at least six months. In that case, testing of neurological and psychological functions should be done to demonstrate resolution of the previous deficits.

General Considerations

Many patients with serious diseases of the nervous system may continue to drive, providing physicians perform regular, informed and sophisticated follow-up examinations and, in some conditions, if patients are reliable in following instructions and taking appropriate medications. Patients with most types of diseases of the nervous system are more likely to have symptoms or increases in dysfunction and impairment as a result of physical exertion, fatigue, lack of sleep and extremes of ambient heat and cold. Therefore, they must exercise greater care than usual when driving under such circumstances.

Being licensed to drive an automobile is not only important socially and culturally but also for some persons it is essential for economic support. The physician may consider recommending use of car pools or public transportation, but in some situations this creates undue hardship. In making recommendations about driving, the physician should take into account the individual's needs as well as the type and severity of the neurological dysfunction and the risk posed to others. For example, if driving to and from work were of great importance in earning a livelihood, a patient with a relatively mild, easily controlled seizure disorder might be allowed to drive sooner than 12 months after a seizure.

Restricting a patient with a neurological condition to driving short distances is not advisable, because most crashes occur within towns and cities, presumably during short trips. In fact, the hazards may be greater during short trips than during long trips, because more traffic and more pedestrians may be encountered. Common sense as well as a knowledge of neurological function and dysfunction should govern the physician's recommendations.

References

1. Rowland, LP (ed): Merritt's Textbook of Neurology (7th ed). Philadelphia, Lea and Febiger, 1984.

2. Van Allen MW, Doege TC (eds): Neurological and Neurosurgical Conditions Associated with Aviation Safety (Special Issue). Arch Neurol 1979; 36:731-812.

3. Browne, TR, Feldman RG: Epilepsy. Boston, Little Brown and Company, 1983.

4. Barrow RL, Fabing H: Epilepsy and the Law. New York, Hoeber-Harper, 1956.

5. Bartels EC, Kusakeiozlu O: Narcolepsy-possible cause of automobile accidents. Lahey Clinic Foundation Med Bull 1965; 14:121-126.

6. Dyck PJ, Low PA, Stevens JC: Diseases of peripheral nerve. Chapter 51 in Baker AB, Baker LH (eds): Clinical Neurology. Baltimore, Harper & Row, 1984.

7. Poser, CM, Paty DW, Scheinberg L, et al: The Diagnosis of Multiple Sclerosis. New York, Thieme-Stratton, 1984.

8. McDowell FH, Lee JE, Sweet RD: Extrapyramidal disease. Chapter 38 in Baker AB, Baker LH (eds): Clinical Neurology. Baltimore, Harper & Row, 1984.

9. Konigsmark B, Weiner L: The olivopontocerebellar atrophies. Medicine 1970; 49:227-241.

10. Drachman DA, Hart CW: An approach to the dizzy patient. Neurology 1972; 22:323-334.

11. Friedman AP: Headache. Chapter 13 in Baker AB, Baker LH (eds): Clinical Neurology. Baltimore, Harper & Row, 1984.

12. Wells CE: Dementia (2nd ed). Philadelphia, FA Davis, 1977.

13. Geschwind N, Benson DF: The aphasias and related disturbances. Chapter 10 in Baker AB, Baker LH (eds): Clinical Neurology. Baltimore, Harper & Row, 1984.

Chapter 7

PSYCHIATRIC DISORDERS

Impairment of driving ability caused by psychiatric disorders may be difficult to assess for two reasons: First, catastrophic events or permanent alterations in functioning are relatively infrequent, and the impairments that occur usually are transient. Second, it may be unclear how alterations in mental state are affecting the driving of a given individual, that is, the effects of impaired attention, judgment and impulse control may be difficult to evaluate without observing the individual's driving behavior. Nevertheless, it is clear that some psychiatric conditions may impair an individual's ability to drive and that certain disorders are especially important in this regard because of their severity or frequency (1,2). These include schizophrenic disorders, paranoid disorders, affective disorders and disorders of alcohol use. In addition, certain types of behavior affect fitness to drive, including aggressive, violent and impulsive behavior. Prevention of motor vehicle crashes depends upon the physician's recognition of persons in these high-risk groups and upon skillful assessments made during the times of their greatest vulnerability.

Schizophrenic and Paranoid Disorders

Patients who have required hospitalization for mental illness have crash rates that are similar to those of patients with chronic medical illnesses but are about twice as high as those of the general population (3). Persons in certain groups, especially those having alcohol use disorders or personality disorders, account for most of the differential, but rates are higher for persons with schizophrenic and paranoid disorders as well (4). Schizophrenia is often disabling, and persons with this illness may require hospitalization during episodes of psychosis. During such episodes, they may experience delusions and hallucinations and their bahavior may be unpredictable and uncontrolled.

Although a psychosis may be temporary, a disturbance of this magnitude may affect the patient's ability to drive. Acutely psychotic patients may be hospitalized for their own protection, and in some states this alone would result in temporary suspension of driving privileges. After the patient's discharge, the physician should assist the patient and family in evaluating the patient's driving ability and should look for signs of stable recovery before advising a resumption of driving. Also, physicians should be mindful that antipsychotic medications may reduce alertness; therefore they should advise patients to limit or avoid driving during initial dose adjustments or periods of sedation. If the dosage of a medication needed to control a patient's disorder is sufficient to slow the reaction time, a test of driving ability may be in order.

Persons with more severe forms of schizophrenia often become withdrawn and show deterioration in their personal habits. Because such patients may be unaware of their limitations, physicians should help responsible family members recognize serious impairment of driving ability and, if it exists, advise against the operation of motor vehicles. When loss of a patient's alertness results in traffic violations or crashes, a physician who recognizes the problem should advise suspension of driving privileges temporarily or permanently. The physician should discuss the problem and recommendations with a responsible family member, noting this in the patient's record.

Alcohol Abuse

Although few studies of drivers involved in motor vehicle crashes have relied on specific criteria for psychiatric diagnoses, it is clear that persons who suffer from alcohol abuse and dependence are over-represented in crashes. Using the criteria of cirrhosis or substantial fatty changes on postmortem examination, Waller and Turkel identified 44% to 62% of drivers involved in fatal, alcohol-related crashes as alcoholics (5). It is estimated that alcoholics are involved in at least one-third of all crashes resulting in death (6).

Because alcoholism is prevalent in the population and the frequency of crashes among persons with this disorder is high, the involvement of alcoholics in motor vehicle crashes, especially those involving fatalities, is substantial. The lifetime prevalence of alcohol abuse and dependence is estimated to be 12% to 16% of the general population (7). A number of studies have shown that alcoholics have crash and violation rates that are roughly double those of the general population of licensed drivers. Also, a large proportion of persons convicted of driving while intoxicated are alcoholics.

The majority of alcoholics who are involved in crashes have high blood alcohol concentrations and are physiologically impaired. In addition, alcohol may release aggressive or other personality tendencies that contribute to the occurrence of crashes. Certain stressful events, such as job loss or divorce, may contribute to uncontrolled drinking and increase the likelihood of a crash or of suicide (8). The physician should be cognizant of the possible effects of such events and, if aware of them, should be prepared to arrange for the patient's treatment or hospitalization.

Treatment for alcoholism is based upon accurate diagnosis, and specific diagnostic criteria are available (9). Traffic violations, including driving while intoxicated and alcohol-related crashes, bring high-risk individuals to the attention of law enforcement authorities and to the attention of physicians treating their injuries. Such individuals should be screened for psychiatric illness and should be referred, when appropriate, for psychiatric evaluation and treatment (10). In addition, physicians should recommend that persons who suffer from alcohol abuse or dependence have their driving privileges suspended until they have abstained from alcohol for a period of three to six months. The same recommendation is made for persons with substance use disorders. Chapter 12 provides a more detailed discussion of the effects of using alcohol and driving.

Affective Disorders

It is not known how often drivers with major depression are involved in motor vehicle crashes. The most serious complication of this condition is suicide, and at one time investigators speculated that motor vehicle crashes might represent atypical or disguised forms of suicide. However, studies have identified few persons believed to have committed suicide among drivers involved in crashes. Schmidt et al determined that fewer than 2% of fatally injured drivers had committed suicide and that fewer than 1% of non-fatally injured drivers had attempted to kill themselves (11).

Although suicide by motor vehicle appears to be rare, physicians should keep this possibility in mind when evaluating the suicidal intentions of depressed patients who may expect to use their motor vehicles. Also, when precautions against suicide are taken, keys to motor vehicles should be removed from the house, as well as knives, guns and medications. When treating persons involved in single-car crashes, the physician should consider the possibility that the crash may have been a suicide attempt. Patients sometimes do not reveal suicidal intent unless directly questioned. When symptoms suggest depression, the physician should inquire specifically about suicidal inclinations.

Affective disturbances by themselves can influence driving ability. Patients with depression and mania suffer from disturbances in attention, judgment and motor activity that can seriously, even if temporarily, affect their fitness to drive. When the physician recognizes impairment of this degree, he or she should alert responsible relatives and, as with suicidal persons, consider hospitalization.

Antidepressant medications may cause drowsiness and postural hypotension. During initial adjustments of dosage, the physician should advise patients to limit or avoid driving.

Antisocial Traits and Personality

Although the term, accident-proneness, has fallen from favor, it is generally conceded that persons with certain personality traits and disorders are over-represented among drivers involved in motor vehicle crashes. In a classic study, Tillman and Hobbs compared 96 drivers with repeated crashes and two groups of drivers without crashes. They found the group of 96 was egocentric, resentful of authority, impulsive and lacking in social responsibility (12); consistent with this personality pattern was a high level of social maladjustment. While the test group was highly selected, the finding of aggression, impulsivity and irresponsibility in persons involved in multiple crashes has been confirmed (13). Unfortunately, personality tests that measure such traits have little value in predicting crashes.

The traits in question are common among young drivers and, to some extent, represent immaturity and lack of socialization. When they exist in one individual, they fit the diagnostic category of antisocial personality (9). There is some evidence that antisocial individuals have increased involvement in motor vehicle crashes. These persons for the most part are young men; they may contribute substantially to the increased crash risk that is known to exist for young males.

The abuse of alcohol or drugs and aggressive or suicidal behavior bring antisocial individuals to the attention of physicians, as do injuries resulting from fighting or crashes. Because persons with antisocial personalities do not have a treatable psychiatric condition and because they are considered legally responsible for their behavior, physicians should not ordinarily recommend suspending their driving privileges on medical grounds. However, if convictions or crashes are part of a pattern of aggressive or irresponsible driving, physicians should communicate their assessment of high risk in support of possible action by licensing agencies. Also, if alcohol abuse or dependence is present in addition to the personality disturbance, a temporary suspension of driving privileges may be recommended. A serious problem is that persons with personality disturbances often continue to drive in spite of having their license suspended or revoked.

Stressful Life Events

Studies linking the onset of illness and life change gave impetus to recent research examining the role of stressful life events in motor vehicle crashes (14). Selzer et al found that more than 50% of fatally injured drivers had experienced interpersonal or vocational stresses during the 12 months preceding their crashes, while less than 20% of drivers in a control group had experienced such stresses (8). Further, 20% of the fatally injured drivers had been acutely disturbed by events occurring within six hours of the crash they caused. A finding by McMurray, that traffic crash and violation rates double six months before and after divorce, provides direct evidence of increased risk of crashes during periods of stressful life change (15).

Patients commonly consult physicians when they are seeking relief of major life stresses. The physician should be aware that interpersonal crises pose physical as well as psychological dangers for the persons involved and that usually stable individuals at those times may become excitable and impulsive and show poor judgment. Excessive use of alcohol or drugs may contribute to their loss of control. In this temporary state, some individuals drive recklessly or otherwise invite serious injury. When they encounter such persons, physicians should arrange promptly for supportive counseling and, if necessary, provide symptomatic relief through the judicious use of medication. Also, physicians should advise against activities that involve risk, like driving, and communicate their concerns to responsible family members or friends.

References

1. Noyes R Jr: Motor vehicle accidents related to psychiatric impairment. Psychosomatics 1985; 26:565-580.

2. Tsuang MT, Boor M, Fleming JA: Psychiatric aspects of traffic accidents. Amer J Psychiatry 1985; 142:538-546.

3. Waller JA: Chronic medical conditions and traffic safety. N Engl J Med 1965;273:1413-1420.

4. Eelkema RC, Bronsseau J, Koshnick R, et al: A statistical study on the relationship between mental illness and traffic accidents. Am J Publ Health 1970; 60:459-469.

5. Waller JA, Turkel HW: Alcoholism and traffic deaths. N Engl J Med 1966; 275:532-536.

6. Waller JA: Medical Impairment to Driving. Springfield, IL, Charles C Thomas, 1973.

7. Robins LN, Helzer JE, Weissman MM, et al: Lifetime prevalence of specific psychiatric disorders in three sites. Arch Gen Psychiatry 1984; 41:949-958.

8. Selzer ML, Rogers JE, Kern S: Fatal accidents: The role of psychopathology, social stress, and acute disturbance. Am J Psychiatry 1968; 124:1028-1036.

9. American Psychiatric Association: Diagnostic and Statistical Manual, Third Edition. Washington, D.C., American Psychiatric Association, 1980.

10. Nathan H, Turnbull J: The psychiatrist's role in combating drunken driving. Can Psychiat Assoc J 1974; 19:381-385.

11. Schmidt CW, Shaffer JW, Zlotowitz HI, et al: Suicide by vehicular crash. Am J Psychiatry 1977; 134:175-178.

12. Tillman WA, Hobbs GE: The accident-prone automobile driver: A study of the psychiatric and social background. Am J Psychiatry 1949; 106:321-331.

13. Donovan DM, Marlatt GA, Salzberg PM: Drinking behavior, personality factors and high-risk driving. J Studies Alcohol 1983; 44:395-428.

14. Holt PL: Stressful life events preceding road traffic accidents. Injury 1982; 13:111-115.

15. McMurray L: Emotional stress and driving performance: The effect of divorce. Behavior Research in Highway Safety 1970; 1:100-114.

Chapter 8

CARDIOVASCULAR DISORDERS

There are no definitive statistical data to establish the roles of specific cardiovascular disorders in impairing drivers and causing crashes. However, the physician frequently can render a responsible opinion on the likelihood that functionally impairing symptoms, such as loss of consciousness or severe chest pain, could cause inability to control a motor vehicle.

The most significant symptom of cardiovascular disorders affecting safe operation of a motor vehicle is loss of consciousness. Any person with a history of loss of consciousness should be advised not to drive until a diagnosis has been established and it has been determined that the condition is a benign one unlikely to recur, or medical control has been instituted making recurrence unlikely according to generally accepted medical criteria. An example of the latter situation is the use of a pacemaker to control syncope secondary to complete heart block.

Cardiovascular conditions, such as valvular disorders, coronary artery disease and congenital disorders, usually can be classified as to functional severity. A person with such a condition is not likely to suffer from sudden incapacitation unless the disorder has an associated rhythm disturbance. Table 1 shows an accepted functional classification for determining impairment of the cardiovascular system.

The physician may wish to estimate the patient's limitations using exercise testing. Table 2 shows the relationship of the patient's energy expenditure to the functional classification given in Table 1 according to the systems used by several investigators (1). The physician should be aware of the marked variations in patients' abilities and in their willingness to cooperate.

Rhythm Disturbances

Cardiac rhythm disturbances vary greatly in their significance and with regard to impairing the ability to drive. Episodes of sudden loss of consciousness, lightheadedness or weakness can occur and seriously impair the driver. For a functional classification relating to rhythm disturbances that may be used by the physician or by licensing officials, see Table 3.

Congenital Heart Defects

Asymptomatic conditions rarely affect safe driving whether or not there has been surgical correction. It is recommended that persons with symptomatic congenital heart conditions, such as those causing cyanosis or pulmonary hypertension, not receive medical qualification in Class I, even if the conditions are controlled by medications. Also, it may be inadvisable for such persons to operate larger commercial vehicles because of the heavy work that may be required. Usually, however, these persons may operate light commercial vehicles and may receive medical qualification in Class III.

Table 1

CLASSIFICATION OF CARDIOVASCULAR IMPAIRMENT *

Class 1: The patient has cardiac disease but no resulting limitation of physical activity. Ordinary physical activity does not cause undue fatigue, palpitation, dyspnea or anginal pain.

Class 2: The patient has cardiac disease resulting in slight limitation of physical activity. The patient is comfortable at rest and in the performance of ordinary, light, daily activities. Greater than ordinary physical activity, such as heavy physical exertion, results in fatigue, palpitation, dyspnea or anginal pain.

Class 3: The patient has cardiac disease resulting in marked limitation of physical activity. The patient is comfortable at rest. Ordinary physical activity results in fatigue, palpitation, dyspnea or anginal pain.

Class 4: The patient has cardiac disease resulting in inability to carry on any physical activity without discomfort. Symptoms of inadequate cardiac output, pulmonary congestion, systemic congestion or the anginal syndrome may be present, even at rest. If any physical activity is undertaken, discomfort is increased.

*Adapted from Criteria Committee of the New York Heart Association: Diseases of the Heart and Blood Vessels: Nomenclature and Criteria for Diagnosis (ed 6). Boston, Little Brown and Company, 1964, pp 112-113. Copyright 1964, Little Brown and Company; reproduced with permission; source, ref. 1.

TABLE 2
RELATIONSHIP OF METS AND FUNCTIONAL CLASS ACCORDING TO 5 TREADMILL PROTOCOLS

	METS	1.6	2	3	4	5	6	7	8	9	10	11	12	13	14	15	16
TREADMILL TESTS	Ellestad					1.7	3.0			4.0						5.0	
						10 PER CENT GRADE											
	Bruce					1.7		2.5		3.4				4.2			
						10		12		14				16			
						3.4 MILES PER HOUR											
	Balke				2	4	6	8	10	12	14	16	18	20	22	24	26
				3.0 MILES PER HOUR													
	Balke			0	2.5	5	7.5	10	12.5	15	17.5	20	22.5				
		1.0	2.0 MILES PER HOUR														
	Naughton	0	0	3.5	7	10.5	14	17.5									
	METS	1.6	2	3	4	5	6	7	8	9	10	11	12	13	14	15	16
CLINICAL STATUS		SYMPTOMATIC PATIENTS															
			DISEASED, RECOVERED														
					SEDENTARY HEALTHY												
							PHYSICALLY ACTIVE SUBJECTS										
FUNCTIONAL CLASS		4			3		2		I and NORMAL								

In the Ellestad protocol, the numbers in the boxes are miles per hour (mph); in the Bruce protocol the top numbers are mph and the bottom numbers are the percent grade. In the Balke and Naughton protocols the numbers are the percent grade.

Adapted from: Fox SM III, Naughton JP, Haskell WL: Physical activity and the prevention of coronary heart disease. *Annals of Clinical Research* 1971; 3:404-432.
Copyright © 1971 The Finnish Medical Society Duodecim
Reproduced with permission. Source, ref. 1.

Table 3

ARRHYTHMIA CLASSIFICATION

Type 1   Benign rhythm disturbances that usually are of no clinical significance:
          Atrial premature beats
          Occasional premature ventricular contractions (PVCs)
          Atrial dysrhythmias of brief duration

Type 2   Rhythm disturbances that are controlled by medication or pacemaker.
          Atrial fibrillation
          Atrial flutter
          Partial or complete A-V block
          Ventricular dysrhythmia or "sick sinus" syndrome

Type 3   Rhythm disturbances that are incompletely controlled, e.g. paroxysmal atrial
          tachycardia. The patient has symptoms other than syncope but is able to
          lead an active life.

Type 4   Documented cardiac arrhythmias with episodes of syncope that are not
          controlled.
          Atrial and ventricular tachyarrythmias
          High degrees of A-V block

Coronary Artery Disease

It is recommended that a person with a history of coronary artery disease be considered to have Class I medical qualifications only if he or she is without symptoms and shows no evidence of ischemia or frequent or complex premature ventricular contractions (PVCs) during a submaximal stress electrocardiogram (ECG). A thallium perfusion study also should be carried out and, in a person having an equivocal stress ECG, the study should show no re-perfusion evidence of ischemia. A 24-hour Holter study may be useful in establishing the presence of silent ischemia. If coronary arteriography is done, it should show no more than 70% occlusion of any major coronary artery except for the left main coronary artery, which should show no more than 50% occlusion.

Persons with angina pectoris that is precipitated by moderate exertion usually may qualify for Class III, but not for Class I or Class II. Angina that occurs at rest or is provoked by minor annoyances or the maneuvering of a vehicle is a contraindication to any type of driving. One should not rely on medications taken while driving, such as nitroglycerin or oxygen, to prevent or eliminate angina that is likely to occur.

Myocardial Infarction, Coronary Artery Surgery, Angioplasty

Following acute myocardial infarction, or either coronary artery bypass surgery or percutaneous transluminal angioplasty (2), an individual may be permitted limited operation of a private vehicle at the discretion of the attending physician. Such an individual may be considered for medical qualification in Class II only after four to six months without symptoms and a normal submaximal ECG.

A driver who has had a myocardial infarction, coronary artery bypass surgery or coronary artery angioplasty should not be considered to be medically qualified in Class I until 12 months after any of those events. To be qualified, the individual should be without symptoms and should show no evidence of ischemia or of frequent or complex PVCs during a submaximal stress ECG. A thallium perfusion study also should be carried out and, in a person having an equivocal stress ECG, the study should show no re-perfusion evidence of ischemia. A 24-hour Holter study may be useful in establishing the presence of silent ischemia. If coronary arteriography is done, it should show no more than 70% occlusion of any major coronary artery, except for the left main coronary artery, which should show no more than 50% occlusion.

Valve Replacement

Persons who have had heart valve replacements usually can qualify in Class III without restrictions; if they remain asymptomatic and under medical supervision, they may be considered for qualification in Class II.

Hypertension

Hypertension for the most part does not cause symptoms and in itself it does not impair the driver, but the complications of hypertension can seriously impair driving ability. Also, the medications used to control hypertension should be evaluated for their impairing effects, especially orthostatic hypotension and sedation. The effects of antihypertensives and other medications are considered in greater detail in Chapter 12.

The following recommendations assume that the blood pressure is determined with several trials.

For Class I medical qualification, the systolic blood pressure should be under 180 mm Hg and the diastolic blood pressure should be under 105 mm Hg.

For Class II medical qualification, the systolic blood pressure should be under 200 mm Hg and the diastolic blood pressure should be under 115 mm Hg.

For Class III medical qualification, driving should be limited only according to the patient's symptoms.

Other Conditions

A person known to have an abdominal or thoracic aneurysm or a large aneurysm elsewhere should not be considered for qualification in Class I or Class II until the aneurysm is treated effectively.

A person with a cardiac pacemaker should not be considered for qualification in Class I or Class II because of the serious consequences of pacemaker failure (8).

References

1. American Medical Association (AMA): Cardiovascular system. Chapter 4 in Guides to the Evaluation of Permanent Impairment. Chicago, American Medical Association, 1984, pp 103-134.

2. Council on Scientific Affairs: Percutaneous transluminal angioplasty. JAMA 1984; 251:764-768.

3. Cardiovascular Problems Associated with Aviation Safety. Eighth Bethesda Conference of the American College of Cardiology. Amer J Cardiol 1975; 36:573-628.

4. Functional Ability in Driving: Guidelines for Physicians. Salt Lake City, Utah State Driver License Medical Advisory Board, 1981.

5. Weygandt JL: Guidelines for interpretation of the cardiac standards for school bus operation in Wisconsin. Proc Amer Assoc Automot Med, 1980, pp 35-44.

6. Kloster FE: Complications of artificial heart valves. JAMA 1979; 241:2201-2203.

7. Waller JA, Naughton TJ, Gibson TC, et al: Methodologic and other issues concerning medical impairment to driving. Proc Amer Assoc Automot Med, 1981, pp 189-200.

8. Phibbs B, Marriott HJL: Complications of permanent transvenous pacing. New Engl J Med 1985; 312:1428-1432.

Chapter 9

RESPIRATORY DISORDERS

Respiratory impairment can interfere with a person's ability to operate a motor vehicle safely by limiting oxygenation of the blood, which can lead to diminished judgment, reduced concentration and even loss of consciousness. However, respiratory impairment only infrequently is the basis for licensing actions. To evaluate those with known or suspected pulmonary conditions, the physician should obtain a detailed history, giving special attention to the frequency and severity of dyspnea, wheezing and coughing and associated lightheadedness. Dyspnea should not be used as the sole criterion for evaluating impairment.

Assessment of respiratory impairment usually should include spirometry, and generally acceptable testing criteria are available (1). Pulmonary function testing is not infallible, and a high degree of patient cooperation is required to obtain accurate and reproducible values. Reproducibility is the best criterion of reliability; it is reasonable to expect two determinations of forced vital capacity (FVC) and the one-second forced expiratory volume (FEV_1) to be within 100 ml or 5% of each other (2). If wheezing or other evidence of bronchospasm is evident, the testing should be done before and after the patient uses a bronchodilator.

Table 1 is suggested for use in evaluating pulmonary impairment (1). It is emphasized that there is no direct relationship known between pulmonary functioning and driving tasks or risk of crashes and that indirect measures must be used until tests can be devised and validated that involve the driving task.

Table 2 represents recommendations for licensing different classes of drivers according to the classes of respiratory impairment shown in Table 1.

It is recommended that a person who has dyspnea when sitting at rest be considered to be qualified only in Class III, and then only after successfully completing a road test. Restrictions of driving related to speed, distance or time of day may be appropriate for a severely disabled driver.

It is recommended that persons with a history of uncontrolled and recurring episodes of severe dyspnea not drive, even though the dyspnea cannot be demonstrated by pulmonary function testing.

TABLE 1
CLASSES OF RESPIRATORY IMPAIRMENT*

	Class 1 0% No Impairment	Class 2 10-25% Mild Impairment	Class 3 30-45% Moderate Impairment	Class 4** 50-100% Severe Impairment
DYSPNEA	The subject may or may not have dyspnea. If dyspnea is present, it is for non-respiratory reasons or it is consistent with the circumstances of activity.	Dyspnea with fast walking on level ground or when walking up a hill; patient can keep pace with persons of same age and body build on level ground but not on hills or stairs.	Dyspnea while walking on level ground with person of the same age or walking up one flight of stairs. Patient can walk a mile at own pace without dyspnea, but cannot keep pace on level ground with others of same age and body build.	Dyspnea after walking more than 100 meters at own pace on level ground. Patient sometimes is dyspneic with less exertion or even at rest.
	or	or	or	or
TESTS OF VENTILATORY FUNCTION**				
FVC FEV_1 FEV_1/FVC ratio (as percent)	Above the lower limit of normal for the predicted value as defined by the 95% confidence interval. (See Tables 2-7 and text in ref. 1 for methods of calculation.)	Below the 95% confidence interval but greater than 60% predicted for FVC, FEV_1 and FEV_1/FVC ratio.	Less than 60% predicted, but greater than: 50% predicted for FVC 40% predicted for FEV_1 40% actual value for FEV_1/FVC ratio.	Less than: 50% predicted for FVC 40% predicted for FEV_1 40% actual value for FEV_1/FVC ratio. 40% predicted for D_{CO}.
	or	or	or	or
VO_2 Max	Greater than 25 ml/(kg·min)	Between 20-25 ml/(kg·min)	Between 15-20 ml/(kg·min)	Less than 15 ml/(kg·min)

* Source: ref. 1.
** FVC is forced vital capacity. FEV is forced expiratory volume in the first second. At least one of the three tests should be abnormal to the degree described for Classes 2, 3, and 4.

Table 2

Respiratory Impairment and Class of
Driver's Medical Qualification

Class of Driver's Respiratory Impairment	Recommended Class* of Driver's Medical Qualification		
	I	II	III
1	yes	yes	yes
2	yes	yes	yes
3	no	yes	yes
4	no	no	yes**

*Classes I, II and III are described in
 Chapter 1.

**A road test may be advisable to determine the person's
 driving capability.

References

1. American Medical Association (AMA): Guides to the Evaluation of Permanent Impairment (2nd Edition). Chicago, American Medical Association, 1984, p. 86.

2. Miller WF, Scacci R: Pulmonary function assessment for determination of pulmonary impairment and disability evaluation. Clinics in Chest Medicine 1981; 2:327-341.

Chapter 10

MUSCULOSKELETAL DISORDERS

Limitations of driving because of orthopedic or musculoskeletal impairment require individual medical assessments in most instances (1-3). Fortunately, few musculoskeletal disorders preclude driving. Adaptive changes in behavior and personal devices and equipment that can be placed in motor vehicles enable operation of vehicles by almost all persons with adequate mental and physical capabilities.

The physician's role is to assess the functional capabilities of the impaired driver and to determine what adaptive devices and training will be necessary to operate the motor vehicle safely (4). Lesser impairments can be managed by the patient and physician without adaptive equipment for the vehicle. If there is a question about the driver's capabilities, a road test may provide useful information.

Braces for the neck, dorsal and lumbar spine, and lower extremities, and limb prostheses can aid driving. Accessories that are available in most new vehicles, such as mirrors, automatic transmissions, and power assists for steering, brakes, door locks, seats, windows and mirrors, can augment the impaired driver's capabilities appreciably.

Selecting adaptive equipment for the motor vehicle and planning specialized driver's training require the advice and participation of an expert in rehabilitation (4-6). Most larger communities have hospitals with rehabilitation units and staff who can evaluate the special needs of impaired patients, select and arrange the acquisition and installation of adaptive equipment for vehicles and provide special training.

With modern technologic developments, a quadriplegic driver may be able to enter, operate and exit the vehicle. Sophisticated adaptive devices for vehicles have become available because of the federal Rehabilitation Act of 1973, which requires that all facilities and programs supported by federal funds be accessible to handicapped persons. Funding of adaptive devices through Medicare and private insurance plans is available to most of the handicapped. Two references may be helpful to handicapped drivers (7,8).

General Requirements

Vehicles equipped with clutches and manual transmissions require that drivers have four functioning extremities. The lower extremities are essential to operate the clutch, brake and accelerator pedals, and the upper extremities are needed to steer and to shift gears.

Drivers utilizing motor vehicles with the usual power accessories and equipment require moderate muscle strength in the extremities that are used to steer, accelerate and brake the vehicles. Also, sufficient range of motion is necessary in the joints of the extremities.

Motorcycle operation requires essentially intact upper extremities and functional lower extremities. Motorcycle operation with a unilateral below-knee prosthesis is possible, but loss of ankle motion requires lifting the entire lower leg to operate the pedal. Sufficient functioning of the hands is necessary for the operator to grasp the handlebar and to operate the front wheel brake lever and the accelerator; operating the latter requires twisting. Adaptive devices are not available for motorcycle controls.

Casts and Braces

Casts that are placed on extremities may temporarily disable patients and affect their driving. Casts on upper extremities impair movement, strength and ability to grasp the controls. An experienced, skillful driver having one functional extremity but otherwise not impaired can operate an automobile equipped with power steering and automatic transmission. A cast on a lower extremity precludes the driving of a vehicle with a clutch.

A patient who has severe limitation of motion of the cervical spine or who is immobilized because of a halo apparatus, a cast about the head and neck or a neck brace or support is impaired and should not drive because rotation of the head and neck and vision are affected. However, some patients, particularly those in soft collars and movable braces, are able to accommodate to the impairment and drive. Drivers with more limited motion might require instruction, the use of side-view and rear-view mirrors and perhaps a test of peripheral vision.

Amputations and Prostheses

Most amputees can operate suitably equipped motor vehicles after proper training. A person with an amputated lower extremity should be trained to use the remaining leg. Persons without either leg should use vehicles equipped with hand controls. If there is an upper and a lower limb amputation, the patient may use an adaptive device to operate the vehicle with an upper extremity prosthesis. Persons who have had both arms amputated may be able to use a prosthesis or adaptive devices enabling them to operate vehicles by using the lower extremities.

Although a person with a below-knee prosthesis may be able to operate the clutch, operating the brakes and the accelerator is more difficult because of the absence of ankle motion. A patient with an upper extremity prosthesis may need an adaptive device to connect the prosthesis to the steering wheel or gear shift.

Recommendations

Drivers who have lost strength or coordination or who have joint stiffness or pain should not be considered to have medical qualifications in Class I unless signs and symptoms are minimal. Although a driver with an amputation or functional impairment of any limb ordinarily would not be qualified in Class I, an exception might be the person with amputation of a leg who operates a vehicle having an automatic transmission.

Under regulations of the federal Bureau of Motor Carrier Safety (9), drivers with the following conditions may not operate commercial vehicles in interstate commerce: impairments of hands or digits that interfere with grasping or grasping with power; impairments of the arm, foot or leg that interfere with the normal tasks of operating a motor vehicle; or any other limb defect or limitation that interferes with operating a motor vehicle.

Drivers with medical qualifications in Classes II and III may have more severe impairments of the musculoskeletal system. The physician's recommendation should take into account the impairment in question and the patient's skills, coordination, strength and driving history and the fact that fatigue occurs more rapidly in persons having weakness of muscles or painful joints.

The more specific recommendations of the U.S. Department of Transportation (USDOT) provide a useful guide (10). These state that to determine the driver's medical qualifications, the muscles of the right lower extremity and those of both upper extremities should be tested for strength, these being the muscles that are most involved in driving. Muscle strength should be determined as follows: right ankle, dorsiflexion and plantar flexion; right knee extension; hip flexion and extension; grip of each hand; each wrist, extension and flexion; and each elbow, extension and flexion.

The USDOT also recommends that the individual's strength with regard to the extremities and joints listed above be graded according to the following scale:

5 - "normal:" complete range of motion against gravity and full resistance.

4 - "good:" complete range of motion against gravity and some resistance.

3 - "fair:" complete range of motion against gravity without resistance.

2 - "poor:" complete range of motion with gravity eliminated.

1 - "trace:" evidence of muscle contraction without joint motion.

0 - "none:" no evidence of muscle contraction.

Depending on the results of the strength testing, the driver should be placed into Group A, B or C as defined below (10), which relates to medical qualifications for operating vehicles as shown in the Table.

Group A - "Good" muscle power in flexion of the right knee; "normal" muscle power at all other joints.

Group B - "Fair" or better muscle power in flexion of the right knee; "good" or better muscle power at all other joints.

Group C - "Poor" or worse muscle power in flexion of the right knee; fair or better muscle power at all other joints.

Table

Muscle Strength and Medical Qualification For Driver's Licensing

Group	Medically Qualified in Class* I	II	III	Unrestricted License	Restricted License	Periodic Re-evaluation
A	yes	yes	yes	yes	no	no
B	no	yes	yes	yes[1]	**	yes
C	no	no	**	**	**	yes

*Classifications of vehicles and drivers' medical qualifications are described in Chapter 1.

**Decisions are made considering the individual's circumstances.

[1]Depends on adaptive equipment in the vehicle.

Source: adapted from ref. 10

References

1. Negri DB: Accidents involving handicapped drivers. Final Report on Contract No. DOT HS-4-00936, National Highway Traffic Safety Administration, U.S. Department of Transportation, Washington, D.C. 20590, March, 1978.

2. Negri DB, Ibison RA: Accidents involving handicapped drivers. Rehabil Lit 1979; 40:149-153.

3. Ysander L: Safety of the physically disabled drivers. Brit J Ind Med 1966; 23:173-180.

4. Less M, Colverd EC, DeMauro GE, et al: Evaluating driving potential of persons with physical disability. Albertson, NY, Human Resources Center, 1978.

5. Colverd EC: Equipment and Adapted Methodologies for Teaching in a Fully Modified Van. Albertson, NY, Human Resources Center, 1983.

6. Koppa RJ, McDermott M Jr, Raab C, et al: Human factors analysis of automotive adaptive equipment for disabled drivers. National Highway Traffic Safety Administration, U.S. Department of Transportation, Washington, D.C., October, 1980.

7. Traffic Safety Department, American Automobile Association (AAA): The Handicapped Driver's Mobility Guide. Falls Church, Virginia, AAA, 1984.

8. Reamy L: Travelability: A Guide for Physically Disabled Travellers in the United States. New York, MacMillan Publishing Co, 1978.

9. Federal Highway Administration, U.S. Department of Transportation: Federal Motor Carrier Safety Regulations, parts 390-397. 42 Federal Register 60078 and following, November 23, 1977.

10. National Highway Traffic Safety Administration, U.S. Department of Transportation: Functional Aspects of Driver Impairment - A Guide for State Medical Advisory Boards. Washington, D.C., U.S. Government Printing Office, 1980.

Chapter 11

AGE AND DRIVING

Without question, drivers in younger age groups are at higher risk of being in crashes and in crashes with serious injuries than are drivers 30 to 65 years old. For example, teenagers comprise 10% of all drivers, but they make up 17% of all drivers in crashes and 16% of drivers in crashes with fatalities. Also, persons 20 to 24 years old comprise 12% of all drivers, but they make up 20% of drivers in crashes and 21% of drivers in fatal crashes (1). Other data indicate that on the basis of passenger-miles traveled in automobiles, pickup trucks and vans, the risk of fatal crashes is highest for very young and very old persons and much higher for young and old males than for young and old females. However, those data do not distinguish between persons who are driving the vehicles and those who are not driving (2).

Persons 65 years old and over comprise 9% of all drivers, and they represent 6% of drivers in crashes and 7% of drivers in fatal crashes (1). However, if one takes into account the fact that older persons drive considerably fewer miles than do younger individuals and tend to drive at less hazardous times of day, the crash record of the older driver per mile driven is seen to be excessive. According to one study, the increase in crash risk among the elderly occurs primarily among those with impairments (3). The number of elderly persons is increasing steadily, and the elderly constitute a growing proportion of drivers (4).

Factors Affecting Crash Risk in the Young

Several factors have been shown to contribute to excessive crashes among young drivers or have been hypothesized to contribute to crashes. The first of these is inexperience with driving. All new drivers are at higher risk of a crash for about two years after licensing, probably because they lack experience. Studies have shown that middle-aged persons who are new drivers also have a high crash risk, but not as high as that of teenagers, which suggests that factors related to youth, such as recklessness, "showing off" or aggression, may be important in the excessive risk.

A method commonly used to overcome the inexperience of youthful drivers is drivers' education programs in high schools. Although this type of approach seems to make sense, the better driving records found in earlier comparisons of drivers who took the courses and those who did not turned out to be attributable to the characteristics of those volunteering for the courses rather than to the courses themselves (5). More recent studies show that, if schools have mandatory drivers' education programs, individuals tend to get licensed at an earlier age. Because those of younger ages at first licensing have higher crash rates during initial years of driving, the overall effect is higher crash rates among teenage drivers in communities with drivers' education programs (6).

Persons less than 25 years old are more likely than older persons to "experiment" with alcohol and to a lesser extent with other drugs. At any given blood alcohol concentration (BAC), young drivers have higher crash risks per mile than do middle-aged drivers (7). The reasons for this are not clear. One hypothesis is that young drivers are trying to learn three behaviors at once: how to drive, how to drink and how to combine both activities. The subject of alcohol is considered in greater detail in Chapter 12.

Psychosocial issues also are relevant. The social interactions that are likely to occur in a vehicle with two or more young occupants have been hypothesized to contribute to the risk of a crash. Schuman et al showed that teenagers who had greater evidence of personal problems also had higher crash rates (8).

Much of the driving that young persons do is recreational, occurring after dark when crash risk per mile is higher. Also, young drivers are more likely to drive older vehicles or vehicles in poorer condition, which could contribute to loss of control of the vehicles (9).

It should be noted that the laws of some states do not permit persons less than 21 years old to perform certain activities, such as driving school buses, on the presumption that those persons lack the experience and maturity needed to carry out such tasks that often put many persons at risk.

Factors Affecting Crash Risk in the Elderly

Higher crash risks of the elderly per mile driven result partly from the physical and mental changes associated with aging. These changes include reduction in night vision and in ability to recover quickly from glare; reduction in overall visual acuity and dynamic visual acuity, that is, the ability to identify an object during motion; some narrowing of visual fields; a yellowing of the lens that decreases color discrimination; reduced ability to do problem-solving under stress; and slowing of reaction time.

Because of reduced night vision and glare resistance, the elderly driver has unique and serious difficulties in driving at night and in making out traffic signs that are improperly placed, have small letters or have poor contrast. The shorter stature of older drivers, especially of older women, means they tend to have less favorable perspectives of oncoming traffic and the road environment.

Pathological conditions that commonly accompany old age also can contribute to problems with driving. These conditions, many of which are discussed elsewhere in this book, include cataracts, glaucoma, optic atrophy, hearing impairment, cardiovascular disease, arthritis, the dementias and problems associated with drugs.

Tending to reduce the risk of crashes of the elderly is the fact that many retired persons, acting either on their own or under advice from their physicians, alter the amount and the type of driving they do. There is evidence that these sorts of adjustments are common among drivers with recent heart attacks (10).

Evaluating the Elderly Patient

It is not uncommon to encounter young drivers with multiple crashes and traffic citations. Such patterns are rare among the elderly, however, perhaps because older persons tend to drive relatively few miles and to drive when traffic density is likely to be lower. Even a single crash or citation for an elderly driver, therefore, may represent a warning that a problem exists. This is especially likely to be the case if the driver has been cited for failure to yield, going through a traffic signal, driving on the wrong side of the road or the wrong way on a one-way street, or driving so as to impede traffic.

In evaluating the elderly person, the physician should determine what medical conditions the patient has and what effect the conditions may have on ability to drive.

Also, the physician should be alert to signals that the patient may be having difficulty with the task of driving, such as a history of getting lost while driving at night or of panicking easily in heavy traffic.

The most difficult question is what to do once the physician decides that an older driver has a problem. The easiest recommendation, and one that can be recommended for many if not for most older drivers, is to avoid night driving and to limit driving to those times of day when traffic is less heavy.

If despite easier driving circumstances, the elderly patient still is an erratic driver, again has a crash for which he or she is responsible or again gets a ticket, it is probably best to recommend stopping driving entirely. In rare circumstances, for example, in rural areas where an individual has no other means of transportation to obtain food or medical care and where, if there is a crash, the patient is unlikely to injure others, the licensing agency might consider permitting the patient to continue driving in spite of the problem. Under those circumstances, the impaired driver would represent only a limited hazard to others.

Because there is such wide variation in individual capability among the adults of any age group and especially among the elderly, recommendations are not given here relating age per se to the driver's medical qualifications and the class of vehicle that he or she is medically qualified to drive. Rather, the decision about the elderly person's driving should be based on the findings in that person and on the associated functional limitations. However, it would be prudent to evaluate persons who are older than 55 years for night blindness if they do much driving of Class I or Class II vehicles at night. Also, persons older than about 60 years who wish to operate such vehicles should be evaluated in relation to the jobs that are involved. For instance, the position may require prolonged driving or strenuous activity; does the patient have sufficient stamina and strength to fill it?

References

1. Statistics Department, National Safety Council (NSC): Accident Facts 1983 Edition. Chicago, NSC, 1983.

2. Carsten O: Use of the nationwide personal transportation study to calculate exposure. HSRI Res Rev 1981; 12:1-8.

3. Waller JA: Cardiovascular disease, aging and traffic accidents. J Chron Dis 1967; 20:615-620.

4. National Highway Transportation Safety Administration: National Highway Safety Forecast and Assessments - a 1985 Traffic Safety Setting. Washington, D.C., U.S. Department of Transportation, 1975.

5. Klein D, Waller JA: Causation, Culpability and Deterrence in Highway Crashes - Automobile Insurance and Compensation Study. Washington, D.C., U.S. Department of Transportation, 1970.

6. Williams AF, Karpf RS, Zador PL: Variations in minimum licensing age and fatal motor vehicle crashes. Amer J Public Health 1983; 73:1401-1403.

7. Hyman MM: Accident vulnerability and blood alcohol concentrations of drivers by demographic characteristics. Quart J Stud Alcohol 1968; 29 (Suppl 4):34-57.

8. Schuman SH, Pelz DC, Ehrlich NJ, et al: Young male drivers. JAMA 1967; 200:1026-1030.

9. Creswell JH Jr: Driver characteristics affecting vehicle condition and response to a motor vehicle inspection program. HIT LAB Reports 1974; 4:1-13.

10. Waller JA, Naughton TJ Jr: Driving and crash experience and ischemic heart disease - implications for countermeasures. 27th Proceedings of American Association for Automotive Medicine, Morton Grove, IL, 1983, pp 249-261.

Chapter 12

ALCOHOL AND OTHER DRUGS

Knowledge about the role of alcohol in crashes and injuries comes not only from laboratory studies and case histories, but also from epidemiologic studies comparing blood alcohol concentrations (BACs) of drivers involved in crashes with BACs of persons driving under similar circumstances but not involved in crashes. Because of these studies, there is little doubt that drinking alcoholic beverages is a major contributor to motor vehicle crashes and the serious injuries that result.

In this publication, measurements of BAC are given in terms of "weight per volume," that is, the number of milligrams of alcohol per 100 milliliters of blood (mg%), as recommended in the Uniform Vehicle Code (1). Such measurements may be divided by 1000 and expressed as <u>percent</u> weight per volume (w/v). For instance, a BAC of 100 mg% is equivalent to one of 0.10% w/v. Both measurements can be made to represent "weight per weight" determinations by dividing by 1.055, a number that represents the specific gravity of blood.

At present, a conservative estimate based on data from the U.S. Department of Transportation (USDOT) is that about 11% of drivers involved in all crashes have BACs greater than 50 mg%; about 8% of drivers involved in crashes limited to property damage have elevated BACs; approximately 17% of drivers involved in crashes with nonfatal injuries and 24% of those in crashes with serious injuries have elevated BACs; about 45% of drivers in fatal crashes have BACs of 100 mg% or higher; and almost 70% of drivers in fatal crashes involving just one vehicle, for which the driver is considered to be responsible, have BACs greater than 100 mg%.

In short, as property damage and the severity of injuries in crashes increase, so does the probability that alcohol is involved. Road users other than automobile drivers also are frequently impaired by alcohol. Recent estimates of alcohol impairment rates for other categories of fatally injured road users are: 43% of motorcycle drivers; 15% of pedal-cycle drivers; 14% of truck drivers; 54% of drivers of recreational vehicles and buses; and 39% of adult pedestrians (2).

Applying these figures nationally and using data from other sources, it is estimated that motor vehicle crashes involving alcohol-impaired drivers or pedestrians result in an annual toll of 22,000 to 24,000 deaths, more than 35,000 permanently impaired persons and about 600,000 injured persons (3). There is some indication that between 1980 and 1984 the role of alcohol in serious and fatal crashes declined (4).

Alcohol and Crash Risk

The risk of involvement in a motor vehicle crash increases as the concentration of alcohol in the blood (BAC) increases. With a blood alcohol concentration of 60 mg%, a driver is twice as likely to be involved in a fatal crash as is a driver without alcohol in the blood; with a concentration of 100 mg% the driver is seven times as likely to be involved; and with one of 150 mg% the driver is more than 25 times as likely to be involved (Figure; 5-7).

Many factors affect blood alcohol concentrations, including the person's weight, proportions of water and adipose tissue, amount and type of food consumed before and

61

FIGURE
BLOOD ALCOHOL CONCENTRATION AND PROBABILITY OF FATAL CRASH*

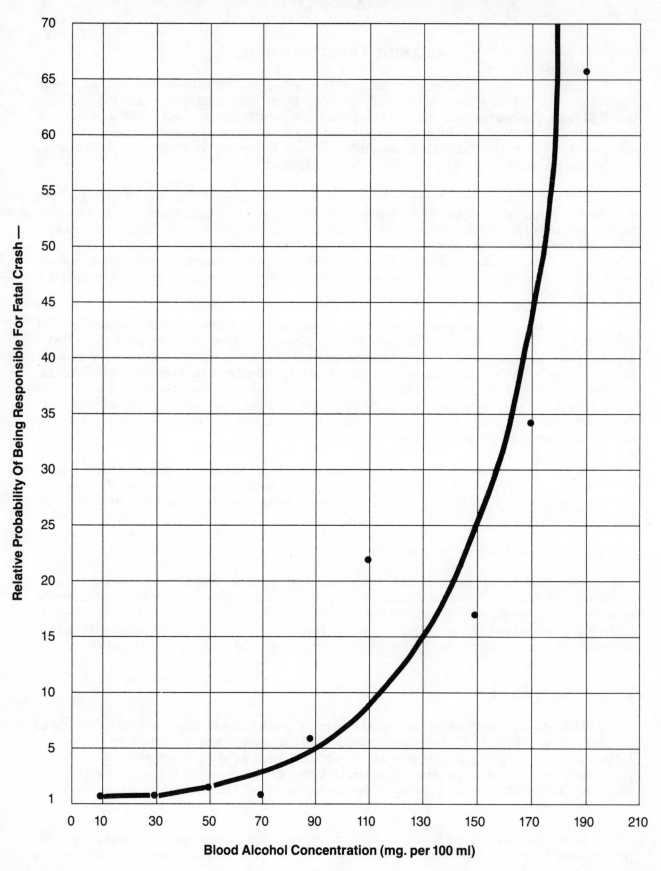

while drinking, rate and amount of drinking, type of alcoholic beverage consumed and concentration of alcohol in the beverage. Some rough approximations of expected blood alcohol concentrations have been developed. Table 1 shows that if a 160-lb person consumes two drinks within an hour, the blood alcohol level will reach 50 mg%, at which substantial impairment begins. After consuming five drinks within an hour, the subject will have a BAC over 100 mg%, the point of extensive impairment and the legal definition of intoxication in most states. Two states and Canada have set the legal limit at 80 mg%.

Distinction must be made between impairment and intoxication. Impairment refers to the presence of a significant decrement in a person's ability to perform a given task when compared with the person's performance if there is no alcohol in the body. Intoxication, a term used by police officers for many years, refers to obvious signs, such as swaying, slurred speech, inability to walk a straight line or difficulty standing. In the person who often drinks heavily, substantial impairment may exist long before the appearance of intoxication (8).

All persons, including heavy drinkers, are considered to be significantly impaired at BACs above 100 mg%. According to the Uniform Vehicle Code (National Committee on Uniform Traffic Laws and Ordinances, Washington, D.C.), persons with BACs of 80 mg% also are impaired. Some individuals do not appear intoxicated until their BACs reach of 200 to 300 mg% (8). Because of the divergence between what exists and what appears to exist, the laws of many states define intoxication as having a BAC of 100 mg% or 0.10% w/v. Some states have a "presumptive impairment" law, under which persons with BACs of 100 mg% or greater are presumed to be "under the influence," unless it can be demonstrated that they were not. Other states have an "impairment per se" law in which a BAC of 80 mg% or 100 mg% or higher is defined as illegal, just as driving above 55 mph has been defined as speeding.

Behavioral impairment at a given blood alcohol concentration varies among individuals. The risk of crash involvement at various blood alcohol concentrations is higher for young than for middle-aged drivers. A young driver with a given BAC is more likely to be involved in a crash than is a middle-aged driver with the same BAC, and the risk of a crash increases more sharply at higher BACs for youths than for drivers of other ages (6,7,9). The reasons for this higher risk are complex but are believed to be related in part to lack of experience with drinking, driving and combining the two behaviors (10).

Infrequent drinkers in all age groups tend to be at higher risk of crash involvement at a given BAC than are frequent drinkers (11). However, the latter individuals are far more likely to drink until they reach high BACs and to do so much more often. Thus, their exposures to the risk of a crash are believed to be greater than are the exposures of impaired infrequent drinkers.

Risk of crash involvement at given BACs also varies by sex. According to one study, women with BACs over 80 mg% were nine times more likely to be crash-involved than were those with no alcohol, while men with BACs of 80 mg% were twice as likely to be crash-involved (7). Despite the higher crash risk of drinking women than of drinking men, more than three-fourths of crash-involved drinking drivers are men, because they drive, and drive after drinking, much more frequently than women.

TABLE 1
<u>APPROXIMATE</u> RELATIONSHIPS OF BODY WEIGHT, NUMBER OF DRINKS
AND BLOOD ALCOHOL CONCENTRATION*

Body Weight (pounds)

No. Drinks** in One Hour	100	120	140	160	180	200	220	240
	Approximate Blood Alcohol Concentration (mg%)							
1	40	30	30	20	20	20	20	20
2	80	60	50	50	40	40	30	30
3	110	90	80	70	60	60	50	50
4	150	120	110	90	80	80	70	60
5	190	160	130	120	110	90	90	80
6	230	190	160	140	130	110	100	90
7	260	220	190	160	150	130	120	110
8	300	250	210	190	170	150	140	130
9	340	280	240	210	190	170	150	140
10	380	310	270	230	210	190	170	160

* Adapted, with permission, from a table of the Utah Alcohol Safety Action Project, 2525 South Main, Salt Lake City, Utah 84115.
** One drink is equivalent to one ounce of 100-proof liquor, a four-ounce glass of table wine or 12 ounces of beer.

Who Are the Drinkers in Crashes?

When the population of crash-involved drinking drivers is examined, two main groups stand out as having particularly high risk: (1) problem or addicted drinkers; and (2) young drivers, particularly young males. Clearly, males less than 25 years old, alcoholics and problem drinkers are significantly over-represented among drinking drivers who get into trouble on the highway.

Alcoholics and problem drinkers are estimated to include about a tenth of the adult population, but they are involved in at least one-third to one-half of all alcohol-related crashes with serious injuries (12). Reducing the remaining half to two-thirds of alcohol-related traffic casualties can be achieved by reducing alcohol-impaired driving among social drinkers, especially young ones.

The second major high-risk group for alcohol-related injuries in crashes, drivers who are 15 to 24 years old, constitute 22% of all drivers but 44% of the drinking drivers involved in fatal crashes (2,3). This is an age at which there is much drinking and much experimenting with heavy drinking. Fortunately, most youths have "settled down" by age 30 years, and there is a reduction in their drinking problems and in their risk of crash involvement.

Dealing With the Alcoholic or Problem Drinker

The presence of alcohol in a person who has crashed or has had a serious injury of any kind should suggest to the physician that the person may have a drinking problem. The higher the BAC, the greater the likelihood that the suspicion will be correct, especially if the patient has a BAC of 150 mg% or higher. Often it is not possible to determine the presence of alcohol or the extent of recent consumption without a BAC determination. Tests for alcohol in the blood are discussed in Chapter 13. The typical patient who has alcohol on the breath already has a BAC of 100 mg% or greater.

One screening method to determine whether a drinking problem exists is to ask the patient specific questions and to make judgments on the basis of several positive answers or on the basis of answers showing inconsistencies. For example, a person may report health problems and difficulties with job or family but may say that regarding alcohol, he or she can "take it or leave it"; or the person may be defensive or unusually nonchalant while answering. A counselor in problems related to alcohol may be helpful in determining if alcoholism is present.

Several reasonably effective mechanisms exist that can help identify persons who may have drinking problems. These include the criteria of the National Council on Alcoholism (13) and the Michigan Alcoholism Screening Test (MAST) (14). Knupfer showed that two questions can identify most people at high risk of problems related to alcohol (15). The questions are: (1) Think of all the times and places when you had something to drink. During the last 12 months, how often did you drink eight or more drinks in a single day? (2) About how often do you drink enough to get "high"? An answer to either question of "once a month" should raise one's suspicion, and suspicion should increase if the answer is "once a week" or more often.

Just as a diagnosis cannot be made unless and until questions are asked, treatment cannot begin unless and until confrontation with the patient occurs, that is, telling the patient about the suspected diagnosis and what the condition is doing or is likely to do.

For the alcoholic who has been identified and confronted, the difficult question is how to predict whether he or she is at high or low risk of alcohol-related crashes. Most persons with uncontrolled alcoholism or drinking problems should not be driving at all.

Persons who become aggressive after drinking, for instance, getting into fights with family members, friends or others, or jumping into their cars and driving, and persons who do much of their drinking outside of the home, are at particularly high risk of involvement in crashes. Persons whose usual pattern is to come home, drink heavily and fall asleep may be at lower risk of injury on the highway but at higher risk of injury at home.

The physician should be aware that the loss of the driver's license, or the threat of losing it, can be powerful leverage to get the patient to confront the alcohol problem and to begin and finish treatment. It is in the best interests of the patient and the public for the physician not to recommend licensing until there is good evidence the patient has accepted treatment, has made substantial progress in it, has not consumed alcohol for at least three to six months and has demonstrated some insight into the problem.

A serious problem for the physician in dealing with alcoholic patients is the difficulty of verifying whether patients' affirmations of sobriety are truthful. Family members often can provide key information.

Recommendations Regarding Alcoholism

Alcoholism is the medical condition most frequently associated with serious motor vehicle crashes in the United States. In one study, 20% of fatally injured drivers of trucks with trailers had BACs of 150 mg% or higher (16). Federal standards for drivers of trucks in interstate commerce require that a person with a history of alcoholism have stopped drinking long enough to recover good judgment and no longer have withdrawal effects or impairment due to alcoholism.

The requirement for drivers in interstate commerce is appropriate for all drivers of vehicles in Classes I and II. In order to meet it, a person should not only have stopped drinking for at least four months, but also show evidence of insight into the nature of, and the reasons for, the alcohol problem. Preferably, the person would have made such progress under the care and guidance of a program or specialist in alcoholism. Also, the individual should not be using any other psychotropic drug for mood control.

In terms of qualification for Class III driving, and assuming that the driver's license is not suspended or has not been revoked, it is recommended that an individual with alcoholism be permitted to drive if he or she has undergone detoxification, has not been drinking for at least 30 days and is currently under active treatment for alcoholism, or has been sober for at least two months, has successfully completed the active phase of treatment and demonstrates evidence of insight into the condition.

Drugs Other than Alcohol

Although less is known about the role of other drugs than about the role of alcohol in highway crashes (18), it is certain that some prescription, over-the-counter and illegal substances have the capability of altering vision, perception, judgment, attention span, motor function and other characteristics that are important in the safe operation of a motor vehicle (Table 2).

Table 2

Classes of Drugs with Potential
For Affecting Driving Skills*

Sedative, Hypnotic, or
Anti-Anxiety Agents

    barbiturates
    benzodiazepines

Analgesics

    codeine
    narcotics
    propoxyphene

Anti-Allergy Agents

    antihistamines

Antipsychotic or
Antidepressant Agents

    cyclic antidepressants
    haloperidol
    phenothiazines

Antihypertensives

    clonidine
    guanabenz
    methyldopa
    reserpine

Anti-Motion Sickness Agents

    antihistamines

Skeletal Muscle Relaxants

    carisoprodol
    dantrolene
    methocarbamol

Ophthalmic Agents (topical preparations)

    Most agents for treating glaucoma

Antibiotics

    minocycline

Drugs and Chemicals of Abuse

    alcohol
    amphetamines (chronic use)
    cocaine (chronic use
    marijuana
    phencyclidine (PCP)

---

* From ref. 19

It would be wise for the physician when first prescribing any drug to discuss with the patient the possibility of adverse reactions affecting alertness, gait, other physiologic functions, or activities such as driving, and the need to notify the physician if they occur (19). Combinations of drugs and combining the use of drugs with the use of alcohol should be of special concern to the physician.

Drugs that have a sedative action as part of their pharmacologic profile usually lose this effect when taken daily over a prolonged period. For this reason, taking anticonvulsant agents with sedative actions should not be a factor in decisions about the driving of patients with epilepsy whose seizures are controlled, unless the dose is sufficient to cause side effects. However, appropriate restrictions should apply for a short period if the dosage is increased or if there is a drug substitution (19).

A study of 440 drivers 14 to 34 years old who died in motor vehicle crashes in urban areas of California indicated that alcohol was present in 70% of the drivers, and marijuana or cocaine was present in 37% and 11% of the drivers, respectively (20). There was no comparison group in the study. The study design, the presence of alcohol, which tended to obscure the role of other drugs, and the small number of cases in which only one drug was present prevented a conclusion about the role of drugs other than alcohol in the crashes. The authors stated that the role of marijuana in crashes should receive further investigation.

There are many case studies of individuals who have crashed or have been arrested for illegal driving behavior while under the influence of various psychotropic or hallucinogenic substances. About 10,000 such arrests occur annually in the United States. Unfortunately, controlled studies on drugs similar to those that have been done with alcohol do not exist (18). Studies of drug levels of fatally injured drivers show that more than 10% of them have drugs other than alcohol present (20), but often these are in combination with BACs of 50 mg% or greater, raising the question as to what extent impairment was due to the other drug, to alcohol alone or to the combination.

Studies to date have not demonstrated a substantial difference between the proportion of the population using drugs at any moment in time and the proportion of drivers in fatal crashes who have the drugs in their bodies (18). Although most investigators in the field believe that some individuals become involved in highway crashes because of drug use, either legal or illegal, the authors know of no firm evidence that any drug other than alcohol contributes significantly.

References

1. Committee on Medicolegal Problems, American Medical Association (AMA): Alcohol and the Impaired Driver. Chicago, American Medical Association, 1968, p XIII.

2. Fell JC: Alcohol Involvement in Traffic Accidents: Recent Estimates from the National Center for Statistics and Analysis. Washington, D.C., U.S. Department of Transportation (DOT HS-806-269) 1982.

3. Statistics Department, National Safety Council (NSC): Accident Facts 1983 Edition. Chicago, NSC, 1983.

4. National Highway Traffic Safety Administration, U.S. Department of Transportation (USDOT): Fatal Accident Reporting System 1983. Washington, D.C., USDOT, 1984, p. 17.

5. Jones RK, Joscelyn KB: Alcohol and Highway Safety 1978: A Review of the State of Knowledge. Ann Arbor, The University of Michigan Highway Safety Research Institute, 1978.

6. Perrine MW, Waller JA, Harris LS: Alcohol and Highway Safety: Behavioral and Medical Aspects. Washington D.C., U.S. Department of Transportation (DOT HS-800-599), 1971.

7. Borkenstein RF, Crowther RF, Shumate RP, et al: The Role of the Drinking Driver in Traffic Accidents. Bloomington, IN, Indiana University Department of Police Administration, 1964.

8. Goldberg L: Tolerance to alcohol in moderate and heavy drinkers and its significance to alcohol and traffic. In Proceedings of First International Conference on Alcohol and Road Safety. Stockhols, Jugelbergs Boktrycheri, 1951, pp 85-106.

9. Farris R, Malone TB, Lilliefors H: A Comparison of Alcohol Involvement in Exposed and Injured Drivers. Washington, D.C., U.S. Department of Transportation (DOT HS-801-826), 1976.

10. Wagenaar AC: Alcohol, Young Drivers and Traffic Accidents. Lexington, Massachusetts, DC Heath and Co, 1983.

11. Hurst PM: Epidemiological aspects of alcohol in driver crashes and citations. In Perrine MW (ed): Alcohol, Drugs and Driving. Washington, D.C., U.S. Department of Transportation (DOT HS-801-096), 1974, pp 131-157.

12. Vingilis E: Drinking drivers and alcoholism: Are they from the same population. In Smart T (ed): Research Advances in Alcohol and Drug Problems. New York, Plenum Publishing Co, 1983, vol 7, pp 299-342.

13. Criteria Committee, National Council on Alcoholism: Criteria for the diagnosis of alcoholism. Amer J Psychiat 1972; 129:127-135.

14. Pokorny AD, Miller BA, Kaplan HB: The brief MAST: a shortened version of the Michigan alcoholism screening test. Amer J Psychiat 1972; 129:342-345.

15. Knupfer G: The risks of drunkenness. Brit J Addiction 1984; 79:185-196.

16. Baker SP: Alcohol in fatal tractor-trailer crashes. Proceedings 19th Annual Meeting American Association Automotive Medicine, 1975, pp 234-243.

17. Bauer RL: Traffic accidents and minor tranquilizers, a review. Public Health Reports, 1984, 99:52-574.

18. Moskowitz H: Guest editor's introduction to Special Issue, Drugs and Driving. Accid Anal Prev 1985; 17:281-282.

19. American Medical Association (AMA): AMA Drug Evaluations (5th ed). Chicago, American Medical Association, 1983.

20. Williams AF, Peat MA, Crouch DJ, et al: Drugs in fatally injured young male drivers. Public Health Rep 1985, 100:19-25.

Chapter 13

TESTING FOR ALCOHOL

Physicians may become involved in legal matters related to testing drivers for alcohol after crashes, and testing for alcohol may be essential for their effective treatment of patients, especially unconscious ones, in emergency rooms or hospitals. Also, results of laboratory tests for alcohol may be helpful in identifying patients who have problems related to alcohol. Thus, physicians should be acquainted with procedures and pertinent state laws related to testing for alcohol.

Results of chemical tests receive strong emphasis in the prosecution of alcohol-impaired-driving cases, especially in states with laws presuming that a stated blood alcohol concentration (BAC) is per se evidence of driving while intoxicated. Generally, the physician is authorized by law to draw blood specimens to test for chemicals; in doing so, he or she should use the following guidelines (1):

1. Usually 10 ml of venous blood is drawn; this should be done expeditiously and without using alcohol to prepare the skin. The physician should be prepared to describe the methods used.

2. Each specimen should be labeled with the full name of the subject or patient, the date and time the blood was drawn, the name of the person drawing the blood, and the initials of a witnessing law officer.

3. The labeled container should be placed in an envelope having the subject's or patient's full name, information about whether the subject was alive or dead when the sample was drawn, the place where the blood was drawn (hospital, jail, etc.), the name of the person drawing the specimen, the date and time it was taken, and the signature of the witnessing law officer.

4. The law officer requesting the laboratory test generally is responsible for filling out forms that establish an unbroken chain of evidence. No unauthorized person should handle the blood specimen.

5. Results of the physician's examination for signs of intoxication should be recorded carefully in any case involving law enforcement, preferably on the report form concerning alcohol that is recommended by officials of the state or county involved. A publication of the National Academy of Sciences reviewed the signs of intoxication (2).

Analysis of the blood sample should be done in accordance with standard laboratory procedures and any requirements of the state's alcohol-impaired-driving laws. The physician who is called upon to testify in a case involving intoxication should prepare thoroughly and attempt to be knowledgeable about all aspects of the case, because the quality of scientific evidence and testimony given at the trial is the most important factor in preventing overturn of alcohol-impaired-driving convictions on appeal.

Analyses of blood samples for ethanol content (3-5) are usually carried out by one of the following methods: (a) chemical reduction of acid dichromate; (b) enzymatic oxidation by alcohol dehydrogenase with colorimetric determination of reduced nicotinamide adenine dinucleotide (NADH); (c) gas-liquid chromatography.

Gas chromatography is the most accurate of the three methods; it can determine the concentration of a variety of substances and volatile toxins in addition to ethanol, including other aliphatic alcohols that may be present in chronic alcoholics and contribute to their symptoms. The less sophisticated dichromate method selectively detects ethanol and other aliphatic alcohols. The enzymatic oxidation method is reasonably but not completely specific for ethanol, having a limited reactivity with methanol and isopropanol.

The physician may wish to determine whether there is a possibility of chronic alcohol abuse. The level of the serum enzyme, gamma-glutamyltranspeptidase (GGTP), is a useful indicator, because its level is usually higher in chronic alcoholics than in acute abusers regardless of the presence or absence of acute intoxication (6).

Although the drawing and preserving of a blood sample in a traffic offense case may be in lieu of or in support of a breath alcohol measurement, analysis of alcohol in the breath is by far the method most frequently used by law enforcement officers to measure blood alcohol concentrations. Breath alcohol measurements are usually carried out by law officers or technicians who are trained and certified in operating the analytical equipment involved. Some state alcohol-impaired-driving laws require a blood alcohol measurement to confirm a breath alcohol measurement, but in other states a measurement of breath alcohol conducted in conformity with established criteria is acceptable as evidence of blood alcohol concentration. With most breath-analyzing equipment, the samples are prepared for preservation as well as analyzed.

The National Safety Council's Committee on Alcohol and Drugs recommends that all breath tests be recorded to three decimal points and reported to two decimal points, and that the lower of the two recorded values be used. Although breath tests are usually conducted by a police officer or technician, the physician should be aware that close attention to quality control in breath and blood alcohol testing is becoming more important in alcohol-impaired-driving cases. As more states pass "per se" legislation, challenges of test procedures by defendants are increasing steadily.

References

1. National Safety Council (NSC): Recommendations of the Committee on Alcohol and Drugs. Chicago, NSC, 1977.

2. Burns M, Moskowitz H: Alcohol impairment tests for DWI arrests. Transportation Research Record no. 739. Washington, D.C., Transportation Research Board of the National Academy of Sciences, 1979.

3. Sonnenwirth AC, Jarrett L (ed): Gradwohl's Clinical Laboratory Methods and Diagnosis. St. Louis, CV Mosby Co, 1980 pp 406-407.

4. Jatlow P: Acute toxicology of ethanol ingestion: Amer J Clin Path 1980; 74:721-724.

5. Kaplan A, Szabo LL (ed): Clinical Chemistry—Interpretations and Techniques. Philadelphia, Lea & Febiger, 1983.

6. Luchi P, Gianpiero C, Alessandro B: Forensic considerations on the comparison of serum gamma-glutamyltranspeptidase activity in acute experimental intoxication and in alcoholic car drivers who caused accidents. Forensic Sci 1978; 11:33-39.

Chapter 14

PREVENTING INJURIES IN CRASHES

Because highway-related injuries are such a serious problem and have major effects on physicians and financial resources, as well as catastrophic effects on the injured and their families, it is fitting that physicians be knowledgeable about measures to prevent injuries. Such an attitude is in keeping with the physician's obligation to contribute to the betterment of the community (1).

Responsible medical practice often involves counseling patients about avoiding risks to their well-being. For instance, a physician may recommend that an infant receive immunizations against poliomyelitis and measles, that a mother have a cervical (Papanicolaou) smear and that a father have his blood pressure measured and his prostate gland palpated. In the same way, physicians should instruct their patients to use safety belts in automobiles, advise parents to use appropriate restraints for their children and strongly advocate helmets and protective clothing for motorcyclists. Also, physicians should be models of good health behavior themselves, utilizing effective preventive measures like the lapbelt-shoulder harness.

Safety Belts, Restraints

Three decades of use in automobiles and dozens of studies have demonstrated the efficacy of safety belts. The restraints, when properly fastened, achieve their effectiveness by preventing occupants' ejections from crashing vehicles and by diminishing or preventing occupants' contacts with the interior components that can injure, such as steering wheels, windshields and hard surfaces and knobs. Effectiveness of the lapbelt in preventing serious injury is about 27% and that of the lapbelt-shoulder harness or three-point safety belt is about 42% (2).

In a study of 28,000 crashes, Bohlin (3) found that 25% to 30% of the vehicles' occupants were using three-point safety belts and estimated the effectiveness of the belts in reducing injuries to be 40% to 90%. Fatal injuries of occupants not using the restraints occurred in crashes throughout the entire range of speeds and at speeds as low as 12 miles per hour, while no person using a restraint was killed in a crash that occurred at less than 60 miles per hour.

Recent evidence indicates that persons thrown out of cars during crashes, or "thrown free," are about 40 times as likely to die as persons who are kept in their vehicles by restraints (4). Also, persons not using restraints are about twice as likely to be rendered unconscious during crashes as those using restraints. Perhaps that fact explains why the proportion of persons dying in vehicular fires, which occur relatively infrequently after crashes, is about six times smaller among persons using seat belts than among those not using them (4).

One study indicated that the costs of crashes to the State of Michigan in 1979 was about $21.5 million (5). The cost of providing medical care to persons injured in the crashes exceeded more than half of that total, indicating that a substantial proportion of the $21.5 million could have been saved through the use of restraints. Total economic loss in the state because of the crashes was about $1.22 billion.

Some type of safety belt always should be used by each occupant when a car is in motion. The shoulder harness should be snugly but not tightly applied to the chest, passing across and over the shoulder. It never should be worn passing under the arm and through the axilla. The lapbelt should be fastened firmly about the hip joints.

The three-point safety belt fits most persons older than four years or weighing more than 40 pounds and having a sitting height of 22 inches (6). When drivers and other occupants use the restraints, they may have improved control of their vehicles and be more comfortable, and they will receive important protection if they crash.

Injuries from Restraints

Injuries related to lapbelts and lapbelt-shoulder harnesses are infrequent and nearly always much less severe than the injuries they prevent (6-8). For instance, a review indicated that, through 1980, there were 11 reported cases of duodenal rupture in persons using seat belts (9). A study of 651 persons in crashes who were using lapbelts showed an incidence of severe abdominal injury of 0.5% (7), which compares favorably with the lapbelt's known efficacy of 27% in preventing serious and fatal injuries (2). Hodson-Walker noted that many seatbelt injuries were in persons wearing the belts too loosely or too high (7).

Christian compared the injuries of 196 persons wearing seatbelts and those of 773 persons not wearing seatbelts (10): 9% of the wearers had severe injuries and 72% had minor injuries; in contrast, 39% of the nonwearers had severe injuries and 57% had minor injuries. Persons not using seatbelts were much more likely to have fractures. While soft tissue damage of the abdominal wall was more likely to occur in persons using seatbelts, the users incurred damage to hollow and solid viscera only half as frequently as nonusers. Injuries of the spine and of the face were much more likely to occur in nonusers. Although 18% of the nonusers sustained severe eye injuries, no person using a restraint had such an injury.

The three-point safety belt, which spreads the immense forces in crashes over a wider area than the lapbelt and allows less flexion of the spine, is considered to be an improvement over the lapbelt (6,7). Specific data are not available, but the rate of serious injuries with that type of restraint probably would not exceed the rate associated with lapbelts, which is 0.5%. In Bohlin's study of 28,000 crashes, users of three-point safety belts had only slight injuries, such as bruises and single fractured ribs (3).

Regarding medical conditions that may be contraindications to the patient's use of a restraint, in 1977 a committee of the American Association for Automotive Medicine concluded that there is no specific contraindication. In 1984, a committee of the Medical Society of the State of New York reviewed studies and experiences to date in the United States and elsewhere and concluded that there should be no specific category of exemption on medical grounds to the use of safety belts.

In 1983, a national commission in England, where using lapbelts is mandatory for passengers in front seats, concluded that a person fit to drive an automobile is fit to wear a seat belt; few medical conditions are aggravated by using satisfactory seat belts; using the belts aids safe control of vehicles; and exemption from using restraints on medical grounds is seldom justified (11).

Pregnancy is no contraindication to using a restraint. According to a study of 208 pregnant women, maternal and fetal deaths were less likely to occur in mothers using lapbelts (12). The authors concluded that the lapbelt exerts its protective effect by preventing the mother's ejection and that pregnant women should use restraints. An expert AMA committee concluded that using the three-point restraint provides important protection to both the mother and the fetus in the event of a crash and that using the three-point restraint is preferable to using the lapbelt alone (13).

Children's Restraints

Several varieties of restraints and safety seats exist for children, and evidence is accumulating that the restraints effectively prevent death and serious injury (14). For instance, one study showed that the efficacy of children's restraints in preventing death in crashes is 93% (15). Not considered in that figure is the fact that properly restrained children are not thrown into other passengers, increasing their risk of injury as well. The child should be harnessed properly into the restraint or safety seat, which in turn should be fastened properly to the vehicle with a seat belt (16).

The restrained infant or small child should ride in the middle of the rear seat, and both doors should be locked. Restraints for children are relatively inexpensive, and those being produced must conform to federal standards. Physicians should attempt to assure that parents use the restraints according to manufacturers' instructions, which increases their efficacy. Many kinds of activities have broadened the use of the restraints: efforts of physicians' groups, hospital staffs, "first-ride" programs and state laws (17).

Motorcyclists and Helmets

Although there may be a downward trend in death rates per 100,000 registered motorcycles in the United States, the number of deaths in motorcycle crashes has increased rapidly in recent years from 759 in 1962 to 4,720 in 1981 (18). In 1962, there were about 660,000 motorcycles in the nation, and in 1981 there were about 6 million. The American Motorcyclist Association estimates that the death rate for motorcyclists per 100 million vehicle miles is about 4 1/2 times higher than for persons using other kinds of vehicles (19).

Approximately 80% of motorcycle crashes involve head injuries (20). Several studies indicate that the motorcyclist's use of a helmet reduces the risk of serious head injury by 50% to 67% if there is a crash. In a study involving four states, motorcycle helmets were associated with a 65% reduction in injuries to the head, face and neck and with a 64% reduction in fatal injuries (21). In persons not using helmets, permanent impairments were more frequent and costs of medical care were higher.

An AMA conference in 1977 concluded that motorcyclists' helmets, for which there are federal and other standards, do not contribute to cervical injuries, nor do they reduce the users' peripheral vision or impair their hearing (20). The use of such helmets, especially those with visors that protect the eyes and face, is strongly urged by the American Medical Association. In addition to using a helmet and properly protecting the face and eyes, the motorcyclist should wear gloves and sturdy clothing that protects all parts of the body. Also, the motorcycle should be kept in good working condition and the motorcyclist should realize that safe operation calls for extraordinary care, experience and skill.

Physicians, persons providing emergency services and others caring for injured persons should have special training in removing helmets, because of the possibility of causing injuries of the spinal column or neck to become more severe. The American College of Surgeons publishes a pamphlet describing the proper way to remove an injured person's helmet (22).

Other Opportunities in Prevention

In addition to advising their patients about restraints and helmets, physicians can contribute to the prevention of injuries by participating in the activities of various community groups and organizations. That such groups can have a significant role is shown by the decrease in deaths from crashes that followed legislators' enactment of a speed limit of 55 miles per hour and by the reduction in children's deaths that followed pediatricians' efforts and legislators' enactment of state laws mandating restraints for infants in cars.

The knowledgeable physician will know which state agencies deal with aspects of the problem of highway safety and where basic information about such programs can be obtained. The physician may have opportunities to apply this knowledge in the workplace, to assist educators, to advise law enforcement or drivers' licensing officials or to serve on committees involved with such agencies. Physicians can participate in voluntary groups that help educate the public. They also can inform colleagues about this challenging problem and help professional groups and medical societies take more active roles in the prevention of injuries and in the proper care of injured persons.

References

1. American Medical Association: Principles of medical ethics. JAMA 1981; 245:2188.

2. Council on Scientific Affairs, AMA: Automobile-related injuries - components, trends, prevention. JAMA 1983; 249:3216-3222.

3. Bohlin NI: A statistical analysis of 28,000 accident cases with emphasis on occupant restraint value. Proceedings of 11th Stapp Conference, 1967, pp 299-308.

4. O'Day J, Scott RE: Myths and realities of seat belt use. UMTRI Research Review 1984; 14:1-12.

5. Flora JD: Traffic accident costs borne by the State of Michigan. Highway Safety Research Institute Research Review 1981; 12:1-8.

6. Synder RG: Automobile safety belts. JAMA 1984; 251:90.

7. Hodson-Walker NJ: The value of safety belts: A review. CMA Journal 1970; 102:391-393.

8. Arndt RD: Cervical-thoracic transverse process fracture: Further observations on the seatbelt syndrome. J Trauma 1975; 15:600-602.

9. Hudson I, Kavanagh TG: Duodenal transection and vertebral injury occurring in combination in a patient wearing a seat belt. Injury 1983; 15:6-9.

10. Christian MS: Non-fatal injuries sustained by seatbelt wearers: A comparative study. Brit Med J 1976; 2:1310-1311.

11. Medical aspects of exemption from seat belt wearing guidelines for practitioners prepared by the Medical Commission on Accident Prevention. J Soc Occup Med 1983; 33:49-52.

12. Crosby WM, Costiloe JP: Safety of lap-belt restraint for pregnant victims of automobile collisions. New Engl J Med 1971; 284:632-635.

13. Committee on Medical Aspects of Automotive Safety: Automobile safety belts during pregnancy. JAMA 1972; 221:20-21.

14. Decker MD, Dewey MJ, Hutcheson RH Jr, et al: The use and efficacy of child restraint devices - the Tennessee experience, 1982 and 1983. JAMA 1984; 252:2571-2575.

15. Christoffel KK, Tanz R: Motor vehicle injury in childhood. Pediatrics in Review 1983; 4:247-254.

16. More detailed information on safety devices and safety seats for children and on restraints for adults is available from Physicians for Automotive Safety, P.O. Box 430, Armonk, New York 10504.

17. Paulson JA: Case for mandatory seat restraint laws. Clin Pediatrics 1981; 20:285-290.

18. Statistics Department, National Safety Council (NSC): Accident Facts 1982 Edition. Chicago, NSC, p 56.

19. Russo PK: Easy rider - hard facts, motorcycle helmet laws. New Engl J Med 1978; 299:1074-1076.

20. Hames LN, Petrucelli EA: Head Protection for the Cyclist. Chicago, American Medical Association, 1977, p 2

21. McSwain NE Jr, Petrucelli E: Medical consequences of motorcycle helmet nonusage. J Trauma 1984; 24:233-236.

22. Committee on Trauma, American College of Surgeons (ACS): Techniques of Helmet Removal From Injured Patients. Chicago, ACS, 1980.

Chapter 15

STATE LEGISLATION PERTAINING TO RESTRAINT SYSTEMS, IMPAIRMENTS AND ALCOHOL-IMPAIRED DRIVING

During recent years there has been much state legislation dealing with automobile safety, especially with issues such as driving while intoxicated, the minimum age at which one legally can drink alcoholic beverages and mandatory use of restraints by children and adults in automobiles.

Since Tennessee passed the first "child passenger protection" law in 1977, all other states have enacted such laws; these mandate that children below a specified age in moving motor vehicles be protected through the use of restraint systems meeting certain standards. In 1978, a resolution adopted by the AMA's House of Delegates directed AMA to "...encourage all state medical associations to consider initiating and supporting legislative activity to mandate the use of seat belts or other motor vehicle crash protection restraints for infants and children." A reduction in injuries of children has occurred since the implementation of these laws (1,2).

With regard to driving while intoxicated, there has been considerable legislative activity, and all states have amended their laws since the end of 1981. The scope of subjects covered by the laws includes provisions imposing stricter penalties for alcohol-impaired-driving convictions, including mandatory jail time and participation in rehabilitation programs; provisions concerning the blood alcohol concentration (BAC) that constitutes a rebuttable or conclusive presumption of drunk driving; and provisions setting forth administrative and judicial reforms designed to lessen the problem of alcohol and crashes.

An unusual action was that of the Montana legislature in 1985. The legislature, citing the need to prevent intoxicated persons from operating vehicles on public roads and its belief that the "Designated Driver Program" offered an opportunity to improve traffic safety, adopted a resolution endorsing the program and encouraging any group of persons participating in activities involving the consumption of alcoholic beverages to designate a member who would refrain from drinking alcoholic beverages and would "operate the vehicle conveying the group, to avoid endangering the lives of others."

These widespread activities are the result of a growing understanding and a national consensus that "drunk driving" is a significant killer of children, teenagers and adults, and that about half of all deaths on the nation's roads and highways involve alcohol and intoxication.

In 1982 Minnesota enacted a noteworthy law on the subject of the voluntary reporting by physicians of patients having "significant impairment affecting their ability to drive." The law states that a physician who makes the diagnosis of a physical or mental condition, which in the physician's judgment will impair ability to operate a motor vehicle safely, may report the person's name and information relevant to the condition to the State Commissioner of Public Safety. Upon receiving the report, the Commissioner is to require the person to be examined.

This law does not refer to intoxicated drivers, but it apparently applies to such persons as well as to those having any other physical or mental condition that impairs ability to drive. Under the law, a physician reporting in good faith would be immune from any liability for making the report; also, no cause of action might be brought against a physician for not making such a report.

In July 1984, New York became the first state to enact a law requiring the use of approved safety belts. Coverage under the law extends to all persons operating motor vehicles in the state. The law requires that the driver of the motor vehicle, all front-seat passengers over the age of four years and all back-seat passengers between the ages of four and ten years be restrained by approved safety belts. All front seat and back seat passengers under four years old must be restrained by approved child passenger restraint systems. The law provides for imposing a fine up to $50 upon anyone who violates it.

The New York law directed the Governor's Traffic Safety Committee to "initiate an educational program designed to encourage compliance with safety belt and safety seat usage laws," with the program to focus on the effectiveness of restraint devices and on the monetary savings and other benefits to the public from the law. Since passage of this law, other states either have enacted statutes mandating the use of safety belts in motor vehicles or are considering mandating use of such belts.

With regard to the problem of young drivers involved in alcohol-related crashes, one method that has lessened the problem in some states is raising the minimum age at which it is legal to drink alcoholic beverages. The Surface Transportation and Uniform Relocation Assistance Act of 1984 (Public Law 98-363) was enacted as an attempt to establish a national minimum drinking age by requiring the U.S. Secretary of Transportation to withhold federal-aid highway construction funds from any state that allows any person under 21 years to purchase or be in public possession of any alcoholic beverage.

Currently, 43 states have established 21 years as the minimum drinking age for all alcoholic beverages including beer and wine; three other states and the District of Columbia have established an age of 21 years as the minimum drinking age for alcoholic beverages other than beer and wine. Information on minimum legal drinking ages in all the states is provided in the Table.

In June, 1984, the American Medical Association's House of Delegates reaffirmed its policy supporting mandatory seat belt and children's restraint utilization laws and supported immediate implementation of a program requiring passive restraints (preferably air cushions) in all new automobiles; supported legislative action to promote availability of effective seat belts in all school buses; and supported legislative action to promote availability of effective seat belts in all motor vehicles in public use, including buses, taxicabs and any other vehicles containing passengers.

In June 1985, the House of Delegates adopted a position supporting a blood alcohol level of 0.05% w/v as being per se illegal for driving and urging the incorporation of that standard into state impaired-driving laws; the House also adopted a position supporting 21 years as the legal drinking age.

MINIMUM LEGAL DRINKING/PURCHASE AGES AND DATE OF LAST
LEGISLATIVE CHANGE FOR THE FIFTY STATES AND THE DISTRICT OF COLUMBIA
Prepared by Department of State Legislation, American Medical Association

18	19	21	18/21 or 19/21 combinations
Louisiana (1948)	Idaho (1972)	Alabama (1985)	* Colorado (1945)
	Montana (1979)	Alaska (1983)	** Ohio (1982)
	Wyoming (1973)	Arizona (1984)	*** South Dakota (1984)
		Arkansas (1925)	
		California (1933)	
		Connecticut (1985)	
		Delaware (1983)	
		District of Columbia (1986)	
		Florida (1985)	
		Georgia (1985)	
		Hawaii (1986)	
		Illinois (1980)	
		Indiana (1934)	
		Iowa (1986)	
		Kansas (1985)	
		Kentucky (1938)	
		Maine (1985)	
		Maryland (1982)	
		Massachusetts (1984)	
		Michigan (1978)	
		Minnesota (1986)	
		Mississippi (1985)	
		Missouri (1945)	
		Nebraska (1984)	
		Nevada (1933)	
		New Hampshire (1983)	
		New Jersey (1983)	
		New Mexico (1934)	
		New York (1985)	
		North Carolina (1985)	
		North Dakota (1936)	
		Oklahoma (1983)	
		Oregon (1933)	
		Pennsylvania (1935)	
		Rhode Island (1984)	
		South Carolina (1985)]	
		Tennessee (1984)	
		Texas (1985) [eff.	
		Utah (1935)	
		Vermont (1986)	
		Virginia (1985)	
		Washington (1934)	
		West Virginia (1986)	
		Wisconsin (1986)	

    * - 18 (3.2% Beer), 21 (Over 3.2% Beer, Wine, & Distilled Spirits)
   ** - 19 (Beer), 21 (Wine & Distilled Spirits)
  *** - 19 (3.2% Beer), 21 (Over 3.2% Beer, Wine & Distilled Spirits)
 **** - Several states (e.g., North Carolina, South Carolina, Georgia) have amended their
        statutory provisions relating to minimum legal drinking/purchase age, expressly stating
        that if at any time the provisions of United States Public Law 98-363 penalizing states
        for permitting persons under 21 years of age to consume alcoholic beverages are repealed
        or otherwise invalidated or nullified, the amended state statutory drinking age
        provisions shall revert to the language they contained prior to amendment.

References

1. Decker MD, Dewey MJ, Hutcheson RH Jr, et al: The use and efficacy of child restraint devices - the Tennessee experience, 1982 and 1983. JAMA 1984; 252:2571-2575.

2. Wagenaar AC: Mandatory child restraint laws: Impact on childhood injuries due to traffic crashes. J Safety Res 1985; 16:9-21.